For 21 years Dr James A. Simpson was minister of Dornoch Cathedral in the Scottish Highlands. During his time there he not only served as captain of the Royal Dornoch Golf Club, but wrote many books, some of which, including this one, topped Scottish bestseller charts. Dr Simpson is a regular contributor to magazines and newspapers, at home and abroad. He is also much in demand as an after-dinner speaker.

In 1992 he was appointed chaplain to the Queen in Scotland. Two years later he was elected Moderator of the General Assembly of the Church of Scotland.

Dr Simpson has long believed that in any lecture, discussion or debate a little comic relief does no harm, no matter how serious the topic may be.

D1150216

By the same author

More Holy Wit

Some of My Favourite Things

James A. Simpson

Steve Savage
LONDON AND EDINBURGH

Steve Savage Publishers Ltd
The Old Truman Brewery
91 Brick Lane
LONDON
E1 6QL

www.savagepublishers.com

This revised edition published by Steve Savage Publishers Ltd 2013

First published in Great Britain by Gordon Wright Publishing Ltd 1990

Copyright © James A. Simpson 1990, 2013

ISBN: 978-1-904246-40-4

Typeset by Steve Savage Publishers Ltd
Printed and bound by SRP Press, Exeter

Apart from any fair dealing for the purposes of research or private study, or criticism or review, as permitted under the Copyright, Designs and Patents Act 1988, this publication may only be reproduced, stored or transmitted, in any form or by any means, with the prior permission in writing of the publishers, or in the case of reprographic reproduction in accordance with the terms of licences issued by the Copyright Licensing Agency. Enquiries concerning reproduction outside those terms should be sent to the publishers.

MIX
Paper from
responsible sources
FSC® C014540

Contents

*To my much loved wife and family with whom
I have enjoyed many a laugh*

Introduction

Sir Harry Lauder, the distinguished Scottish singer and comedian, told of a lady who had listened for a whole evening to his jokes and patter, without a hint of a smile ever crossing her face. The next day she confided to a friend, 'He's a great comic. It was all I could do to keep from laughing.' Perhaps she thought it was not really ladylike to laugh out loud. Or perhaps her Calvinistic upbringing had convinced her that for a religious person, tears were more appropriate than smiles and laughter.

How mistaken this is. Many of the greatest saints of the church have practised a religion that had a deep and joyous laugh in it. The capacity to laugh is one of God's most precious gifts. Adversity being present in the world, God may have sought to balance it by giving us a sense of humour. Humour helps us think the unthinkable and accept the unacceptable. It relaxes muscles and relieves stress. Kindly laughter is good therapy. A smile is a curve which can set many things straight.

Nothing gives a readier clue to a person's character than samples of what he regards as witty and worth a laugh. That being so, this book will inevitably provide readers with an insight into my make-up. But more than that, it highlights some of those things that have greatly enriched my life – my native land, my home-town, my family, the church, books, golf, food... As Julie Andrews would say, 'These are a few of my favourite things.' Though in the ensuing pages, I poke fun at all of them, I hope the brief introduction to each chapter will make it abundantly clear how much poorer my life would be without them.

I cherish the remark of the little boy who had been reprimanded for laughing out loud in class. 'Please Miss, I was just smiling and the smile busted.' If this little book, like its predecessor *Holy Wit*, produces a few smiles, and if occasionally these smiles 'bust' into hearty laughter, the time involved in compiling ... and revising it will have been well spent.

The royalties from this book as from my other books will go to support further research into Cystic Fibrosis.

James A Simpson
"Dornoch"
Bankfoot

Playing with Words

Words are much more than just vibrations in the air or little black marks printed on paper. The varying shapes that we call letters, arranged in endless combinations, are the medium we use to express our inmost thoughts and feelings.

We ought never to speak of 'mere words'. Words have the power to brighten or darken people's lives, to make them laugh or cry, to put a spring in their step or cause sleepless nights. Many like Mark Twain can 'live for months on a compliment'. Critical words on the other hand cause countless disputes and divorces.

My favourite kind of humour is that which appeals to the mind its well as the feelings. I admire the clever way advertisers play with words. I smiled recently at a sign in the window of a shop which specialised in maps. It read, 'Feeling disoriented. Why not drop in for a chart?'

A breakdown truck belonging to an A G Peters carried the slogan, 'If your car Peters out, call Peters out.'

I also enjoy the intellectual athleticism of accomplished after-dinner speakers, their penetrating observations and amusing descriptions of everyday situations, their clever one-liners. By way of letting his audience know that his speech was nearing an end, one such speaker said, 'As Lady Godiva remarked at the end of her famous ride, "I'm drawing near to my close".' That appealed to my sense of humour.

Readers of this book will quickly discover that the more 'head' there is in humour, the more I enjoy it.

Conceit is a form of I-strain.

Money is the loot of all evil.

A clear conscience is a result of a bad memory.

Sales resistance is the triumph of mind over natter.

Comic relief is when the life of the party goes home.

An egotist is one who is always Me-deep in conversation, or a conceited ass who thinks he knows as much as you do.

Childish games are those at which your wife beats you.

A bigot is a person who just won't believe you are right.

A self-made man is a bad example of unskilled labour.

Patience is the ability to put up with people you would rather put down.

Politics is the art of foretelling what will happen tomorrow, next month, next year, and being able to explain why it didn't happen.

A beautiful woman is one you notice. **A charming woman** is one who notices you.

A gentleman is a man:

– who calls a spade a spade without adding any qualifying adjectives.

– who when alone at home uses the butter knives.

– who has never heard the joke before.

– who though he gets sleepy in company, never shows it.

Perfection is an infinite capacity for taking pains, and giving them to others.

Insomnia is what a man has when he lies awake at night for an hour.

A playboy is one with whom a girl should eat, drink and be wary.

Romance is oceans of emotions surrounded by expanses of expenses.

A honeymoon is coo-existence – the thrill of a wife-time.

Life is what happens when you are making other plans.

High heels are arch enemies.

A folk-singer is someone who sings about the joys of the simple life using a £3,000 sound amplification system.

Youth is that part of life when you are always looking for greener fields. **Middle age** is when you have given up looking for greener fields because you can't even mow the one you have.

An after-dinner speech is an attempt to wake up the audience after the chairman has concluded his introductory remarks.

Late middle age is the age of metal, the time of life when you have silver in the hair, gold in the teeth and lead in the feet.

Modern art: pigments of the imagination.

Confusion: one woman plus one left turn. **Excitement:** two women plus one secret. **Bedlam:** three women plus one bargain.

Whereas **Baloney** is the unvarnished lie laid on so thick you hate it, **Blarney** is flattery laid on so thin you love it.

Courtesy: a form of polite behaviour practised by civilised people when they have time.

Gardening: soil sport.

Spring: when budding branches cast shadows of impending bloom.

Home: where a man is free to say anything he pleases because no one pays attention to him.

The dining room: the place where the family eats when the painters are decorating the kitchen.

Retirement (a wife's point of view): twice as much husband for half as much money.

Religious awakening: what takes place after the preacher ends his sermon.

Independent TV: where the law of the jingle prevails.

Teenagers are people who:

– express a burning desire to be different by dressing alike.

– get hungry again before the dishes are even washed.

– believe in free speech (their mobile package has to include free calls and free texts).

Christmas is a:

– time when the world breathes a great sigh of belief.

– time for exchanging a lot of things you cannot afford for a lot of things you don't want.

– holiday when neither the past nor the future is of as much interest as the present.

– season when we get children something for their father to play with.

Cricket: a game in which you have two sides, one out in the field, one in. Each man goes in, and when he is out, he comes in, and the next man goes in until he is out. When they are all out, the side that has been out in the field comes in, and the side that was in goes out, and tries to get those coming in out. When they are all out, including the not-outs, that is the end of the game.

Drama critic: one who leaves no turn unstoned.

Rush hour: when the traffic is at a standstill.

Car sickness: the feeling you get every month when the car-payment falls due.

A commuter: a travelling man who pays short visits to his home or office.

A pedestrian: a man with one car and an adolescent son.

Today: the tomorrow you worried about yesterday.

Traffic light: a trick to get pedestrians halfway across the street safely.

A woman driver: a person who drives the same way a man does, only she gets blamed for it.

A jury: twelve persons chosen to decide who has the better lawyer.

Advertising: the science of arresting the human intelligence long enough to get money from it.

Fan Club: a group of people who tell a pop star he is not alone in the way he feels about himself.

A synonym: a word you use when you can't spell the word you first thought of.

A bore: a person who can change the subject back to his topic of conversation, faster than you can change it back to yours.

A newspaper editor: one who separates the wheat from the chaff and prints the chaff.

Babies are angels whose wings grow shorter as their legs grow longer.

Righteous anger is jealousy with a halo.

An opportunist is a person who, given one and two, sees a way to make 12.

The old are the chronologically gifted.

Inflation is a way of cutting a ten-pound note in half without damaging the paper.

A phrenologist is one who likes to press ahead.

Perforation: a rip-off.

Door: what the dog is perpetually on the wrong side of.

The Wonder of Books

For Groucho Marx books were a means of escaping from the dominance of the 'eternal rectangle'. 'I find TV very educational,' he said. 'When someone turns on the set, I go into another room and read a book.'

For Thomas Macaulay, the nineteenth-century writer and statesman, books were among his most treasured possessions. 'If anyone would make me the greatest king that ever lived, with palaces and gardens and fine dinners and coaches and beautiful clothes, on condition that I would not read books, I would not be a king.'

That expresses my own feelings. My life would be greatly impoverished without books. I find it extremely difficult to pass a bookshop or library. I am glad that at an early age I was introduced to books like *Treasure Island* and *Gulliver's Travels*. I can vividly recall also reading for the first time Dickens' *A Tale of Two Cities*, with its unforgettable beginning, 'It was the best of times, it was the worst of times. It was an age of wisdom, it was an age of foolishness.' The ending was even more unforgettable. 'It is a far better thing I do than I have ever done; it is a far, far better rest that I go to than I have ever known.'

Matthew, Mark, Luke and John – these four books, which relate the greatest love story ever told, have enriched many lives. They have blessed the beds of pain, disappointment and bereavement which humanity has lain on. Biographies record what people have done, thought, achieved or been. Other books introduce us to the wonders and glories of the natural world. Novels transport us to distant places, or back in time. They help us escape for a little from the daily routine. Once when the times between the courses of our evening family meal were considerably longer than usual, I discovered my wife reading in the kitchen a few more pages of a novel in which she was engrossed.

For both of us, finding an interesting or exciting new book is like gaining a new friend.

God cannot alter the past, but history books can.

A rare book is one that comes back after you have lent it.

A classic is a book everyone has heard about but which few people have actually read.

Anybody who corrects all his mistakes is probably writing his autobiography.

Asked to contribute to a symposium on the books that most influenced his life, one man submitted two – 'My mother's cook book and my father's cheque book.'

An author who was extolling his many virtues and achievements, paused momentarily and said, 'But enough of talking about myself. Let's talk about you. What do you think of my latest book?'

One critic commented, 'Thank you for sending me a copy of your book. I will waste no time in reading it!'

Another critic, the Rev Sydney Smith, said, 'I never read a book before reviewing it. It prejudices me so!'

A young priest was driving home one night after a very busy day. Suddenly it occurred to him that he had not said his daily offices. So he pulled the car into the side of the road. Discovering that his courtesy light was not working, he jumped out and in the light from the headlights, knelt down with his prayer book. A lorry pulled up and the driver asked him if he was having trouble. 'No,' said the priest, 'everything's fine.' 'Well all I can say,' said the lorry driver, 'is that must be a mighty good book!'

While signing copies of his book *Six Crises*, Richard Nixon asked customers to whom he should address the inscription. One customer, with a big smile on his face said, 'You've just met your seventh crisis. My name is Stanislaus Wajechzleschkl.'

'Why don't you buy a dictionary?' asked the man whose friend repeatedly asked him how to spell certain words. 'What use would a dictionary be?' was the reply. 'If I can't spell the words, I couldn't find them in the dictionary, and if I can spell them, I don't need a dictionary.'

A Browning addict asked the poet the meaning of an obscure passage in one of his books. 'When I wrote that,' replied Browning, 'only two people knew what was meant – God and Robert Browning. Now only God knows.'

The physicist Leo Szilard once remarked to his friend Hans Bethe that he was thinking of keeping a diary. 'It would not however be for publication; I am merely going to record the facts for the information of God.' Bethe replied, 'Don't you think God already knows the facts?' 'Oh, ja, He certainly knows the facts, but He does not know *my* version of the facts.'

The American naturalist Henry David Thoreau had his first book printed at his own expense in an edition of 1,000 copies. Four years later less than 300 had been sold. He bought the remainder with the comment, 'I now have a library of over 900 volumes, over 700 of which I wrote myself.'

The insistent wife of the author of a successful novel said to Professor Brander Matthews of Columbia, 'Haven't you read John's book? You must read it right away. It's great. It will endure.' 'In that case,' he replied, 'there's no real hurry.'

A university librarian tells how after one of his assistants checked in a book, she handed it to him, saying, 'This book is obviously no good. It's entitled *How to Read Better and Faster* and it's been handed in two weeks overdue.'

A certain writer had compiled a book which included without acknowledgement, many of Bertrand Russell's ideas. The plagiarist asked Russell if he would write an introduction. After reading the completed text, Russell's brief reply was, 'Modesty forbids.'

An old lady who saw *Hamlet* for the first time came out complaining that it was full of quotations! When we have no idea what we are talking about and declare, 'It's Greek to me!' we are quoting Shakespeare; if we insist our lost dog has vanished 'into thin air', we are quoting Shakespeare; and if we narrowly avoid being run over and call the errant driver 'a blinking idiot', we are quoting Shakespeare.

An Englishman startled Mark Twain by saying, 'I would give £10 not to have read *Huckleberry Finn*'. While Mark Twain was still reeling from this extraordinary remark, the Englishman smiled and added, 'So that I could have the pleasure of reading it again for the first time.'

Professor Arthur Gossip, the author of several books of sermons, told how in Ireland one summer, he went to the local Presbyterian Church in the morning. To his surprise, but not to his delight, he heard the minister deliver one of his own published sermons. Shaking hands with the minister at the door, Professor Gossip thanked him for the worship service. Then he added, 'I liked your sermon, but I must confess I really liked it better when I preached it myself.' 'Oh,' beamed the minister, 'do you use the same book as I do?'

There are two main reasons for reading a book – one that you can enjoy it, the other that you can boast to everyone about having read it.

Early in my ministry when summer holidays approached, I would pack some weighty theological volumes. I even took a theological book with me on my honeymoon, a newly published book on the parables by Helmut Thielicke. The obvious inappropriateness of the title for honeymoon reading did not occur to me – *The Waiting Father*.

After assigning for study *The Canterbury Tales*, the English lecturer told her class that they would study the whole work with the exception of 'The Nun's Priest's Tale'. 'That,' she added, 'is far too provocative.' At the start of the next session, she announced, 'Let us now discuss "The Nun's Priest's Tale".' The class was prepared. All had read it.

The best way to get a book read is to forbid it.

Some believe the reason why Cain turned out so badly was that Eve had no book on child psychology.

The reason the Bible commands us to love our neighbours and our enemies, is that often they are the same people.

King David and King Solomon led merry, merry lives,
With many, many lady friends and many, many wives.
But when old age crept over them,
With many, many qualms,
King Solomon wrote the Proverbs,
And King David wrote the Psalms.

A Mr Creegan of Merseyside tells how he came across some well-worn and rather dusty illustrated encyclopaedias, treasured from his childhood. They were in a cupboard which he was clearing out. Reluctant to throw them away, he put them on a shelf in his greenhouse. Some time later, his small grandchildren found them and spent many happy hours looking at the pictures. These same books were however, the cause of his most embarrassing moment During afternoon tea with the local vicar, a young voice piped up, 'Grandpa, can we go and look at those dirty books you keep in the greenhouse?'

The excitement books can engender is nowhere better illustrated than in a remark of a dear old lady who was travelling with a copy of *Pride and Prejudice*. She was overheard saying to her friend, 'Please tell me if she marries Mr Darcy, because if she does not, I am not finishing the book.'

When Jimmy Reid, the famous red Clydeside union leader, stood (successfully) for the rectorship of Glasgow University, he was asked which university he had attended. 'Govan Public Library,' was his reply.

Pancakes and Toast

I am glad Pancake Tuesday has a place on the Christian calendar. Although 'Life is more than food', and gluttony a deadly sin, a good well-presented meal can be an enriching experience. Taste is one of our five God-given senses. A fine palate is, I believe, as much the gift of God as an eye that discerns beauty and an ear that appreciates music.

I vividly recall, as a youngster, toasting bread by the open fire on a Sunday night. The long toasting fork was held at the right distance from the coal until the bread, which was impaled on the fork, was golden brown. For perfect taste the slice had to be reasonably thick, beyond the blockage level of a modern toaster. Very quickly there were crumbs on the floor, butter on our chins, and smiles on our faces.

I also recall helping my mother make pancakes on the girdle. My sister and I would coax her to make a few in the shape of animals. The taste of these fresh pancakes was as wonderful as the smell.

It is the social aspect of a good meal that I find most appealing – sitting down with friends and chatting, laughing and reminiscing as we eat. The alternative approach to eating, that of the animals – going off alone into a corner and stuffing yourself with food, has little appeal, no matter how nutritious the food.

To lose my sense of taste would be a considerable loss, but to be separated from the family and friends in whose company I love to eat, would be an even greater deprivation.

A famous statesman was once asked how he arranged the seating of the notables who attended his dinner parties. He replied, 'I don't bother about who sits where. Those who matter don't mind and those who mind don't matter.'

'I rang for ice, but this is ridiculous,' said Madame Talmage Astor as she was helped over the rail of the *Titanic*.

Excessive drinking doesn't improve conversation. It alters the mind so that you are pleased with any conversation.

A delightful cartoon depicts Adam and Eve being expelled from the garden. Adam is saying to Eve, 'If you hadn't insisted on me having my vitamin C.'

A hangover has been defined as 'The wrath of grapes'.

Beside a field of potatoes was a notice which read, 'Twinned with pommes de terre'.

An item on the restaurant menu read, 'The Chef's Special'. Below it one of the diners had written, 'Perhaps he is, but his food is awful.'

Disraeli's description of a dinner: 'Everything was cold except the ice.'

The quality of the meals offered in one hospital canteen was a constant source of aggravation. On one occasion two young surgeons, having looked over what was displayed, reached the same conclusion. 'This calls for a culinary by-pass' – and they left.

An American visiting Britain commented on how he wished they could get such tea in America. 'Look,' said a

Britisher, 'we sent you a whole boatload and you threw it in Boston Harbour.'

A shepherd turning down the offer of a drink from a fellow herdsman said, 'No, Angus, I never drink when I'm droving.'

The Rev Sydney Smith, who loved to eat, said, 'Hell is eating tough mutton. Heaven is eating paté de fois gras to the sound of trumpets.'

Trying to start a class discussion on the topic of friction, the science lecturer asked the class, 'Does anyone know what keeps the cork in a wine bottle?' 'Self-control,' replied one student.

> The left-overs are too few to save
> And a little too much to dump,
> There being nothing to do but eat it,
> Is what makes many mothers plump.
> George Galbraith.

The new epicurean outlook seems to be: 'Eat, drink and be merry for tomorrow we will diet.'

Probably nothing in the world arouses more false hopes than the first day of a diet.

How is it possible for a 2lb box of chocolates to make you gain 5lb?

Rich foods are like destiny – they shape our ends.

Sign in health centre: 'Overweight? It could be just your *desserts*.'

A diet is something you keep putting off, while you keep putting on.

Notice in restaurant: 'Our dishes will take your *breadth* away.'

'Lord if you cannot make me thin, then Lord, make my friends look fat.'

The doctor had put one of his pregnant patients on a strict diet. He had also asked her husband to keep a close eye on what she ate. One day she made a chocolate gateau for her husband's birthday. He ate half of it. The following day she sneaked a bite of it. She enjoyed it so much that before long she had eaten the rest of it. She could only think of one way of keeping it secret. She quickly made another gateau and ate half of it.

A man reading about an 'Eat all you want' diet said to a friend, 'I knew there would be a catch. You have to jog seventy miles a day!'

The young lad looked at the prices on the menu, then turned to his date and said, 'What will you have, my plump little doll?'

The late Henry Ford was once asked by a young reporter what he considered the chief disadvantages of great wealth. 'Well,' said Mr Ford, 'for me it was when Mrs Ford gave up cooking.'

A lady tells how her 14-year-old son and 12-year-old daughter had offered to make lunch. When the thick soup refused to pour from the tin, inspiration struck big brother, and he quickly ran the tin-opener round the bottom of the container, pushing the contents through. Having watched him, his sister then said, with a gleam in her eye, 'Now try adding a canful of water.'

As well as being great competitors in the whisky industry, Mr Dewar and Mr Bell were also great friends.

The story is told how they met one day for lunch in a Perth hotel before going on to the funeral of a common business friend. Mr Dewar ordered two Dewar's whiskies from the bar. Later Mr Bell went to the bar and also ordered two Dewar's whiskies. When asked why he had not bought his own brand of whisky, Mr Bell is reported to have said, 'You don't want to go to a funeral smelling of real whisky, do you?'

Notice in London *Times*: 'A Help The Poor committee met for lunch today and resolved to have another luncheon.'

A Middlesborough mother opened her weekly order from the butcher and found the meat was not the usual good quality. Returning to the shop she showed it to the manager, saying she regretted having to bring it back as normally she was very satisfied. 'Don't apologise,' said the butcher, 'if you were to deliver anything to my home which I found to be unsatisfactory, I would certainly return it to you.' 'I'm afraid that would be impossible,' she said. 'I'm the new midwife.'

Woman to her husband as they leave an exclusive restaurant: 'Try not to think of it as a £140 bill. Think of it as a delightful gastronomic experience.'

A small boy's idea of a balanced meal is a piece of cake in each hand.

When you eat in some restaurants these days you need an after-dinner mint – like the one in Llantrisant!

Did you ever notice that when it comes to restaurants, the lower the lights the higher the prices?

A London lady tells how just one other coat, an expensive-looking mink, hung beside her modest coat in the cloakroom of the exclusive restaurant where she had just had lunch. The waiter, who had seen her come in, selected her coat and helped her into it. She asked ruefully how he had known which coat was hers. His diplomatic reply was: 'Madam would never wear mink at lunchtime.'

A chef is a man with a big enough vocabulary to give soup a different name each day.

George Galbraith highlights a housewife's dilemma:

> What shall I cook? That is the question.
> What I like affects his indigestion.
> What he likes makes my allergies strike,
> And we are fed up with what both of us like.

A couple who were dining in an elegant restaurant had carefully studied the large menu. Not wanting to embarrass himself by mispronouncing the entrée, the husband pointed to the *Suprême de Volaille à la Normande* then said to the waiter, 'I'll have the chicken please.'

'Sir,' said the waiter, 'that is not chicken. That is a capon breast marinated in a dry white wine and simmered in cider with sausage.' As he proceeded rather haughtily to the neighbouring table, the husband noted that he had written just one word on his order pad – 'chicken'.

A tourist who had ordered afternoon tea, received two bits of bread, a butter pat, a cake and a minute portion of honey. Pointing to the honey, he said to the waitress, 'I see you keep a bee.'

One of Dornoch's bachelor worthies had bought a chicken for his evening meal. Having prepared it and put it in the oven, he adjourned to the nearby 'local'. There he got 'detained' as we say in the Highlands. It was after 11 o'clock before he got home. The following morning he told a close friend, how the previous night he had put a chicken into the oven and had taken out a blackbird!

Andy Rooney, a former star of American television, was quoted as saying, 'I don't eat in a restaurant that has a sign outside saying *Home Cooking*. If I wanted home cooking I would eat at home.'

To illustrate that excessive drinking is alas sometimes synonymous with Highland hospitality, a friend told of a Highlander who was coming out of the licensed grocer's with three loaves and five bottles of whisky. 'John,' said a passer-by, 'what on earth are you needing all that bread for?'

When a Highlander was asked if he liked water with his whisky he replied, 'Only if there is room.'

A very old man from Crieff
Ate nothing but prime Angus beef
'It is so juicy and tender'
He explained to the vendor
'I manage quite well wif few teef.'

At a party, the hostess, who had never before opened a bottle of champagne, was struggling with the cork. It popped out suddenly, showering champagne over the gown of one of the guests. The hostess was speechless. However, the soaked guest saved the day by announcing, 'At last I have been launched.'

A tourist stopped at an inn in a small French village and ordered a couple of scrambled eggs for lunch. Afterwards he noted with astonishment that he had been charged an extortionate price for them. 'Are eggs scarce here?' he asked, 'Non monsieur,' said the hotelier, 'eggs are plentiful, but tourists are scarce.'

An American lady once gave a party for Winston Churchill. The buffet was cold fried chicken, an American tradition which the aging statesman found greatly to his liking. He came to her for a second helping. 'May I have a breast?' he asked.

'Mr Churchill,' replied his hostess, 'in this country we ask for white meat or dark meat.' 'I'm sorry,' Churchill replied. The next day the hostess received an orchid. A card bore the handwriting of the great man himself. 'I would be obliged if you would pin this on your white meat.'

Alistair Gillies, the Scottish singer, tells of a friend who owned a hotel on the West Coast of Scotland. One summer he employed a Glasgow University student as a wine-waiter. One day a guest came to him and said, 'That's a most charming waiter you have, but do you realise he has a strange habit? When he brings the wine he pours a little into the glass, and then he picks up the glass and tastes it before saying, "It's very nice".' One wonders what state the student was in by the end of the night!

Fish and chips wrapped in newspaper is a popular British meal. During the conference season, two conferences were being held simultaneously in Bournemouth, one for Newspapermen and the other for Fish and Chip merchants. At the opening session of the Fish and Chip merchants' conference, their secretary suggested that a telegram of good wishes be sent to the newspaper conference, for as he added, 'Our business is wrapped up in theirs.'

A visitor with a thick Scandinavian accent arrived at the Wick Tourist Information Centre and enquired hopefully, 'Fish 'n' Chips?' The seasonal staff member, a helpful soul, gave him directions to the nearest 'chippy' which was just round the corner. After a few minutes, the Norseman reappeared with the same question. Thinking he had misunderstood the original directions, the assistant took him outside and repeated the directions. Off he went, only to return soon afterwards, minus haddock supper, but still enquiring, 'Fish 'n' Chips?' Clearly he had missed the entrance to the 'chippy', so the staff member took him to the shop and there announced triumphantly, 'Fish 'n' Chips'. 'No,' said the Scandinavian, suddenly finding more fluent English, 'Fishing ships.' A rather red-faced assistant pointed in the direction of the harbour and beat a hasty retreat.

A minister's wife, who was harassed by a sudden influx of visitors, asked the youngest member of the family to say grace in the absence of her husband. 'But Mummy, what shall I say?' asked the perplexed youngster. 'Just say what Mummy says,' encouraged his mother. So the child lifted up his voice. 'O Lord, why did all these people have to come to supper on a day like this?'

A diet is what helps a person gain weight more slowly.

The Same Model

On his fiftieth wedding anniversary Henry Ford was asked the formula for a successful marriage. He replied that it was the same formula that had made his motor-car successful. 'Stick to the same model.' Those who today live by the philosophy of touch and go miss so much.

On that fateful night when Abraham Lincoln was shot, he was sitting with his wife in the Presidential box at the theatre. Seconds before the assassin's bullet struck, his wife had coyly asked him what people would think if they could see them sitting there holding hands. Periodic doses of intimacy are no substitute for such an enduring relationship, one in which there is warmth, companionship and joy. Real happiness is being married to your best friend. One of the saddest aspects of modern life is that it seems almost fashionable to go through a marriage breakdown.

I am deeply grateful that for the past fifty years, one part of my life has been unchanging. The young wife who knew me when I had a full head of hair, a slim figure, a good memory and a low golf handicap, knows me now when I am bald, not so slim, forgetful and have a much higher golf handicap. The fact that she still loves me is one of my greatest blessings.

Marriage is:

— a process of finding out what sort of man your wife would have preferred.

– a form of aerobic exercise, requiring much bending and flexing.

– a place of learning, where a man loses his bachelor's degree without acquiring a master's.

– like making a call. You go to adore, you ring a belle, you give your name to a maid, and then you are taken in!

Marriage, said the Rev Sydney Smith, resembles a pair of shears, so joined that they cannot be separated, often moving in opposite directions, yet always punishing anyone who gets between them.

A marriage proposal is a speech often made on the 'purr' of the moment.

A Husband is:

– one who lays down the law to his wife, and then accepts all her amendments.

– one who stands by you in troubles you would not have had, if you hadn't married him.

– one who thinks twice before saying nothing.

– one who when he gets sick and miserable, makes everyone else miserable too.

If you want your wife to pay attention to what you are saying, address your remarks to another woman.

On an application for employment, beside the question 'marital status', one job-hunter wrote: 'Not speaking.'

Your marriage is in a pretty good state if the only person who ever tells you where to go is your travel agent.

Every married man should forget his mistakes. There is no use two people remembering the same things.

A perfect marriage would be between a blind wife and a deaf husband!

G K Chesterton told of an older man who, late one night at a party, sat down next to a pretty young lady. 'May I sit and talk to you,' he said. 'I'm very tired and I want my wife to take me home.'

At a business dinner, a middle-aged man spent twenty minutes talking to an attractive girl. Later his wife remarked to him that she had been very impressed. 'You mean that I can still chat up the birds?' he asked. 'No,' came the reply, 'that you can hold your stomach in for so long.'

The trouble with New Year resolutions is that your wife remembers them.

'How good of God,' said Samuel Butler, 'to allow Thomas and Jane Carlyle to marry each other, and so only make two people miserable instead of four.'

A little incompatibility in marriage is the spice of life – provided the man has the income and the wife is pattable.

One way for a husband to learn about 'do-it-yourself', is to criticise his wife's housekeeping.

The trouble about looking for the perfect wife is that she is usually looking for the perfect man.

A famous will contains the sentence 'My overdraft at the bank goes to my wife. She can explain it.'

What problems wives have – though they don't have an inch of wardrobe space, they have often nothing to wear.

Bishop George Reindrop of Salisbury was a doctor of divinity. His wife was a doctor of medicine. In the diocese they were known affectionately as 'Body' and 'Soul'.

A lot of friction on the highways is caused by half the drivers trying to go fast enough to thrill their girl friends, and the other half trying to go slow enough to placate their wives.

The girl was beginning to fall in love with a young man who was renting the flat attached to her parents' house. 'Stay away from him,' her mother advised. 'I'm willing to bet he's a married man.' 'But mother, he says he is single.' 'I don't care,' said her mother. 'Every time he pays me he turns his back when he opens his wallet.'

A minister once suggested to a reticent Scotsman who was concerned about how harassed his wife was, that he should tell her from time to time that he loved her. On going home his wife poured out all her troubles. He listened well and then said, 'Never mind Mary, I love you.' 'Oh mercy me,' said Mary, 'and noo after sic a day ye come hame drunk.'

A farmer's wife tells how her car had not been washed for some time. She was upset one morning to find that someone had written on the boot: 'Wash me please'. She was comforted, however, when she saw on her husband's car – which was even dirtier – the words: 'Plough me'.

Wanting to please his nagging wife who had given him two ties for his birthday, John went and put one of them on. When he appeared in the kitchen, she took one look at the tie and said, 'What's wrong with the other one?'

A father once told his wife he was certain his son had taken money out of his pocket. When she asked how he was so certain, that it might, for example, have been her, he shook his head. 'No, there was some left.'

When the Highland minister went to call on a lady in his congregation, he found her retired husband leaning on the gate smoking his pipe. This surprised him, for it was a bitterly cold day. When the minister asked him why he was standing outside, he replied, 'Oh the chimney's smoking.' The minister then proceeded to the open door. As soon as he stepped in, he got a dish cloth square in the face. When he finally came out, he tapped John on the shoulder and said, 'John, my chimney sometimes smokes too!'

A Mrs Thompson tells how her mother-in-law always sends her and her husband an anniversary card. It always arrives a day early. She also phones on the right day. Once Mrs Thompson asked her the reason for the early card. 'I know John has a memory like a sieve,' she said. 'But when he opens that anniversary card, he knows he has twenty-four hours to buy something for you.'

George Burns recalls how when his sister fell out with her husband, she returned to the family home. She said, 'Mamma, I'm teaching Charlie a lesson. I'm coming to live with you.' Mrs Burns replied, 'If you really want to teach Charlie a lesson, you go home and I'll come and live with you.'

The bride wanted to get married on a Friday, but the bridegroom insisted on Thursday. His argument was, 'If we get married on a Friday, our silver wedding will fall on a Monday, and that's my darts night.'

A lady who works in a card shop, received a call from a young woman who had ordered wedding invitations just a few weeks before. She asked if it was too late to make a few changes. When the lady asked for details so that she could check with the printer she was told it was a different date, a different church and a different man.

An MP once complained to Ernest Bevin about the absenteeism in war factories among women whose men were home on leave from the services. Bevin, whose great strength was that he understood ordinary people, replied, 'That's not absenteeism, that's human nature.' He later saw to it that women were given leave for such occasions.

A man's wife had to be away from home for two weeks. During the fortnight he learned just how well she knew him. When he reached the second last of the stack of clean plates, he found a note which read, 'Start Dishwasher'.

One is accustomed to humorous birthday cards, Valentine cards and get well cards, but not to humorous wedding invitations. One exception was, 'Clare and Robert, who both said they would never marry, invite you to join them in eating their words.'

We are told in the Book of Kings that Solomon had 'seven hundred wives and three hundred concubines'. I suppose the only thing that could be said in defence of this kind of marital nightmare, is that for Solomon marriage was an instrument of diplomacy. If a neighbouring king thought of making war against him, the court scribe would warn, 'Your Majesty, Solomon is your son-in-law.'

A husband was due to meet his wife at Vancouver Airport. This meant he had to stop at the border between America and Canada, where he was asked why he was entering the country and how long he was planning to stay. He explained that he was picking up his wife at the airport after her trip to Britain. In the same businesslike tone, he was asked two more questions, 'Is the house clean?' and 'Are there flowers in the hall?'

Some wives have unique ways of getting things done. For several weeks one wife had been asking her husband to mend the doorbell, without success. Her final solution was to hang a metal pie dish and a large metal spoon on the door. Needless to say, he got the message.

When a husband declared that he did not want any of the trifle his wife had made, she said, 'But you like sponge, jam, jelly and custard. You are such a fuss.' When after consulting his dictionary their son informed them that the word 'fuss' means 'one who worries about trifles', they all laughed.

On his return home from a meeting, the fond wife asked her husband, 'How was your talk tonight?' 'Which one,' he retorted, 'the one I was going to give, the one I did give, or the one I delivered so brilliantly to myself on the way home in the car?'

'Darling I do love you,' said the middle-aged widow, 'and I would like to marry you. But it frightens me to hear that you have been married five times before.' 'Oh,' he said, 'you mustn't listen to a lot of old wives' tales.'

Most weddings are happy. It's trying to live together afterwards that causes all the problems. Sylvia Harney, in her book *Married*, explains how once in the heat of battle she said to her husband, 'I was crazy when I married you.' He quickly replied, 'Yeah, and I was so infatuated I didn't notice.'

Just as a middle-aged couple were going to sleep, they smelled smoke. The husband jumped out of bed, went out into the hall and rushed back to the bedroom. 'The whole back of the house is on fire!' he cried. They scurried frantically into a hall filled with thick smoke. After what seemed an eternity, they reached the front door. As the husband opened it, he glanced at his wife and saw a smile on her face. 'Good Lord!' he cried, 'What have you got to smile about now?' 'I can't help it,' she replied, 'this is the first night we've been out together in five years.'

A middle-aged man, famous for constant complaining, a nuisance to everyone who knew him, inherited a lot of money. After observing that it wasn't as much as he thought it should be, he told his wife, a gentle, sweet-spirited woman, that he thought he would buy some acreage for them to enjoy in their retirement 'What do you think I should name the spread?' he asked. She replied, 'Why don't you call it *Belly Acres*?'

A multi-millionaire was being interviewed about his self-made fortune. 'I never hesitate,' he said, 'to give full credit to my wife for her assistance.' When asked how she had helped, he replied, 'Well, I was curious to see if there was any income she could not live beyond.'

John Carroll of the *San Francisco Chronicle* told the story of Morris who was dying. Sadie was by his side. 'Sadie,' Morris said in a hoarse whisper, 'remember how we started that little grocery store in Kiev and the cossacks drove us out and you were by my side?'

'Yes,' Sadie said.

'And remember how we had the little vegetable stand in Berlin and the Nazis drove us out, and you were by my side?'

'Yes,' Sadie said.

'And remember how we had the meat market in the Bronx and the mafia took over the neighbourhood and our store was fire-bombed and you were by my side?'

'Yes.'

'And remember how we came to Miami and I had my heart attack, and you were by my side?'

'Oh yes, Morris!'

'Sadie,' Morris said, 'there's one thing I've always wanted to ask you, and now that I'm dying, I can finally ask it.'

'What is it, my darling?'

'Sadie, are you a jinx?'

An advert in the *Yorkshire Evening Post* did not mince words: 'Man offers marriage proposal to any woman with ticket for Leeds United v Sheffield United promotion game. Must send photograph (of ticket).'

A man who was teaching his wife to drive said, 'Go on green, stop on red and slow down when I turn white.'

The actress Joyce Grenfell and her husband Reggie had lively senses of humour. During the Second World War, Joyce had travelled extensively entertaining the troops. While visiting the United States shortly after the war she received a telegram from her husband in England. 'CLEM SAYS GEORGE WISHES TO GIVE YOU THREE QUARTERS LENGTH ROBE, REGGIE.' She guessed that Clem must be Clement Attlee and that George was probably King George VI but it took her some time to realise that three-quarters of the word

'ROBE' was OBE. She was being honoured for her work with the soldiers.

Couples today might do well to adopt the motto that used to be inscribed in wedding rings: 'Be to his virtues very kind. Be to his faults a little blind.'

The actor Franchot Tone was granted a divorce from his wife on the grounds that she *embarrassed him* in company. Commenting on this court case, a Dr Luccock said, 'This decision profoundly affects the whole domestic scene. In future wives will probably not be able to say or do certain things.

'**1.** She will not be able to say, "I've heard that one before dear." Of all the sad words those take the prize. A husband's highest pride is always as a raconteur, a teller of tales. To be stopped in full flight in the middle of a masterpiece, is an embarrassing deflation. Edwin Booth played Hamlet countless times. Why should not a husband recount as often the drama of when he put a traffic policeman in his place?

'**2.** A wife will not be allowed either to interrupt or correct her Master in company. No longer will she be able to say, "You're wrong sweetheart. That didn't happen at Majorca. It happened at Ibiza."

'**3.** She will not be allowed to reveal publicly that her husband is a liar. She will not be allowed to break in on a tense climax by exclaiming, "But we were never in Moscow, darling! How could Stalin have been talking to you?" She will have to remember that imagination is a divine gift, and not wither it!'

A truly happy marriage is one in which a woman gives the best years of her life to the man who made them the best.

No Place Like Home

Though my parents were not wealthy, they were rich in love. Ours was a happy home where family games were played, picnics planned and fancy-dress costumes made when the occasion arose. My mother smiled with her eyes when we presented her with a freshly picked bunch of buttercups and daisies. My father laughed when we told him our childish jokes.

The words 'Home' and 'Family' have always been precious to me. Today we use the word 'automation' to describe the technological process that does the work while we just sit there. When I was young we called this 'Mum'. It was not however until I became a parent myself that I really came to appreciate all that my parents had done for me.

Being a parent is no bed of roses. It involves wiping runny noses, changing nappies, untying knots in shoe-laces, teaching children they are too young to do certain things and too old to do others – never an easy lesson to learn. Parenthood can be very demanding, especially when the little kittens become cats, with all the emotional toil of the teenage years. As a parent you just hope and pray that you do and say the right thing more than half the time.

There is no doubt that the home is the best place to start on any agenda for social improvement. What strengthens the family strengthens society. When the family falters, something very precious is lost. Young people sometimes become outlaws because the gang is the only place where they find the acceptance they should have found at home.

The best thing a father can do for his children is to go on loving them and their mother.

The stork gets blamed for many things which with greater justification should have been blamed on the lark.

During a conversation between Churchill and General Montgomery, the General quoted the proverb, 'Familiarity breeds contempt'. 'I would like to remind you,' said Churchill, 'that without a degree of familiarity, we could not breed anything.'

Birth notice for a first baby: 'Baby flawless, mother breathless, father legless.'

The excited young father wanted to do everything right. Before leaving the hospital with his wife and new baby, he asked the doctor, 'What time will we wake the little fellow up in the morning?'

A woman with eighteen children, who entered Britain's 'Housewife of the Year' contest, was invited to say what quality she most admired in a man. She was quick to reply, 'Moderation'.

Over two decades, the birth of a child to the Campbell family became an annual event on the Island of Skye. Mrs Jessie Campbell now has twenty fine children. She and her husband John belong to the very strict Free Presbyterian Church, a church which accepts every word of the Bible as the word of God, to be obeyed by church members. Local legend has it that a doctor once advised John to desist from having any more children, pointing out that the Biblical command to populate the earth, 'to go forth and multiply', was not intended to be achieved by one man!

Sidney Ascher remembers the young mother of triplets who was being congratulated by her friend. 'Oh yes,' she said, 'we're so happy. It was really fantastic because you know it only happens once in 10,000 times.' Her naive friend thought for a moment and then said, 'That's fantastic, but for the life of me, I can't see how you found time for your housework.'

After a Tory MP had risen in the House of Commons and moved that the House should congratulate Prime Minister Margaret Thatcher on becoming a grandmother, a left-wing Labour MP got to his feet and said that he would go along with that, but then he added, 'I hope the baby will become as good a "crawler" as the proposer of the motion.'

Having just become a proud father, a man decided to open a savings account for his new daughter. Filling up the application form, he was puzzled by the space marked 'occupation'. He said he was tempted to write 'Town Crier'.

Dave Barry tells how all babies have three moods.
Mood One: Just about to cry.
Mood Two: Crying.
Mood Three: Just finished crying.
The job of parents is to keep baby in Mood Three as much as possible. He then reminds us of the traditional way of achieving this. 'When the baby starts to cry, you and your spouse should pass it back and forth repeatedly and recite these words in unison: "Do you suppose he is hungry? He can't be hungry, he's just eaten. Maybe he needs to be burped? No that's not it. Maybe his nappy needs changing? No, it's dry. Do you think he's hungry?"And so on until the baby can't stand it any more and decides to go to sleep.'

Parents know how bedtime prayers can be full of surprises. One little lad, smarting after punishment, finished his prayers with the usual blessings for all the members of the family save one. Then turning to his father he said, 'I suppose you noticed you were not included.'

Parents spend the first part of a child's life getting him to walk and talk, and the rest of his childhood getting him to be quiet and sit down.

A small Indian boy appeared one day in the class of a Lambeth School. The teacher asked him his name. 'Vankatarataam Narasimha Rattaiah,' he said. When she then asked, 'How do you spell it?' he replied, 'My mother helps me.'

When my wife was a little girl she returned home late from school one day. When her mother enquired why she was late, she explained that she had been kept in because she couldn't spell her name. (Her maiden surname was McCorquodale.) When her mother then asked if any others had been kept in, she replied, 'Yes, Laura Farquharson.' It's an unfair world!

'Lord,' said the little boy in his prayers, 'if you can't make me a better boy, don't worry about it. I'm having a real good time as I am.'

All credit to the little boy who, after tumbling down the stairs, picked himself up, smiled and said, 'Well, I was coming down anyway.'

Credit also to the lad who was standing near a box of apples outside the grocer's. When the grocer finally asked, 'Son, are you trying to steal my apples?' he replied, 'I'm trying not to.'

A mother who had been out hanging up her washing found, on returning to the kitchen, her little boy bandaging his finger. On hearing that he had hit it with a hammer, she said, 'But that must have hurt? I didn't hear you crying.' 'No,' he replied, 'I knew you were out.'

'Johnnie, I've told you for the thousandth time, stop exaggerating.'

A man like myself, with five children, is more content than a man with a million pounds, for a man with a million pounds still wants more.

A Cardiff man tells how his wife once held a coffee morning for her new neighbours. Suddenly the door opened and their four-year-old son entered, covered in dust from head to toe. His mother gasped, 'Adrian, what have you been up to?' The little angel replied, 'I've been playing under your bed, Mummy.'

A little boy who had just started school came home one day and announced that he had a girlfriend. 'Jean and I are in love.' Surprised at his use of the term, his mother asked how he knew. 'She told me,' he replied casually.

Of one awful child it was said, 'Even his imaginary playmates won't play with him.'

> Little children surely
> Age you prematurely
> Though if all be told
> They keep you young when old.

At the outbreak of a severe storm, a mother rushed upstairs to calm her little boy, who she was certain would be frantic with fear. But instead, she found him looking out of the window, his eyes bright with excitement, shouting as every clap of thunder sounded, 'Bang it again God. Bang it again!'

An unbreakable toy is one children use to break other toys.

You can learn many things from children – for instance, how much patience you have.

Children's toys would last much longer if grown-ups were given some of their own to play with.

Beneath a roadside notice informing motorists that they could pick their own strawberries, was a light-hearted postscript. 'All children will be weighed on arrival and departure.'

You can always tell a house with a five-year-old in it. You have to wash the soap before you use it.

Attached to the flowers which arrived from her teenage son for Mother's Day, was a note, 'With all my love and most of my allowance.'

A mother tells of the time her teenage daughter and two friends, as well as wearing bleached jeans and way-out hairstyles, had acquired their father's pullovers and T-shirts. One week they received an invitation to a fancy-dress party. They were wondering what to wear when her husband came in. He listened to their wild ideas and then said, 'Why not go dressed as girls?'

Father to teenage son one Saturday morning, 'No you can't use the car, but please feel free to help yourself to the lawn-mower.'

Mothers discipline their children at the rate of several nots per hour.

Two things in life I have had and ample,
Good advice and bad example.

Advertisement in student newspaper. 'Sweet little old lady wishes to correspond with six-foot student with brown eyes answering to initials JDB.' It was signed, 'His mother.'

Overhearing his mother talking one day to her pot plants, a son said, 'I bet they are laughing up their leaves at you.'

An interviewer asked a high-powered executive, 'Have any of your boyhood dreams been realised?' 'Yes,' he replied, 'when I was a little boy and my mother combed my hair, I always wished I didn't have any.'

A couple were making the most of the fine weather catching up on the gardening. Noticing the absence of their teenage daughter, the father called to her inside the house, 'Why not come and help us make the garden look pretty?' It worked. Five minutes later she appeared, dressed in a bikini and carrying a sun-lounger.

A father confided in a friend that he kept all his valuables in the bathroom. 'With three teenage daughters, there is no way a burglar will ever get in there.'

They had been studying in school Darwin's theory of evolution. When James got home he asked his mother, 'Is it true that my ancestors were monkeys?' 'I can't honestly tell you,' said his mother. 'I didn't know your father's people.'

Mother to teenage girl wearing the shortest miniskirt, 'I didn't say your slip is showing, I said your hip is showing.'

After an exam one girl prayed: 'Please God make Copenhagen the capital of Japan, even if it's only for a week or so.'

A father was trying to help his teenage daughter with her homework. The daughter was patient as only children can be with their parents. But finally she closed the books, looked at him compassionately and said, 'Daddy, we might as well face it. You've helped me as far as you can.'

Some teenagers feel that once they have passed their driving test they should pass everything else.

Old lady to grandson in sports car: 'Don't put your foot down too hard on the exhilarator.'

Harassed mother: 'I feel like a six-piece pie being served to ten people.'

A teenager who returned home with his father's damaged car in tow, said, 'At least, Dad, you've not been pouring these car insurance payments down the drain.'

A teenager, with the questionable help of his Dad, was struggling with his geography project on Africa. Zimbabwe, Malawi and Chad all figured in the questions. 'Let's see now,' said the father, 'what were these countries' maiden names?'

Two friends met after many years. They were filling each other in on their news. 'Did I tell you about my grandchildren?' asked George. 'No,' said Sam, 'and I certainly appreciate it.'

On a television show, in an exchange about embarrassing moments, Jack Ford, son of former President Gerald Ford, remembered a visit to the White House by the

Queen. 'I was all excited and anxious to meet her,' Ford recalled. 'Hurrying to get into my formal clothes, I couldn't find dress studs for my shirt and rushed to Dad's room to look for some. Having no luck there, I ran down the corridor and pressed the lift button to return to my room. As the lift opened and I stepped in with my shirt unfastened, I found myself with the Queen, Prince Philip and my mother and father. As mother turned to introduce me, the Queen simply said, "I've one just like that!"'

A woman who had seven children, all of whom had turned out well, was asked by an adoring friend, what method she had used to bring them up. 'Method!' she replied. 'Method! I've had seven methods.'

A little five-year-old girl who didn't want to go to school was finally persuaded by her father that there was nothing to be afraid of, and that if she didn't like it she could always leave when she was sixteen. On her first day as her father made to leave the classroom, tears began to form. 'Don't forget to come for me when I'm sixteen.'

Three little boys, who were camping for the first time, were heard talking. 'There's a stone under my sleeping bag,' said one. Another moaned, 'That's nothing, I'm trying to sleep on a hard root. I wish I was home in my soft bed.' 'Me too,' cried another, 'I'm cold and thirsty. Let's go home.' 'Are you crazy?' said the obvious leader of the group. 'If we go home now, they'll never let us do this again.'

At the end of her first week at school, one five-year-old announced, 'I'm wasting my time. I can't read, I can't write and they won't let me talk.'

A Dr Caldwell, who had just retired, tells how his grandson in England asked his mother rather anxiously, 'Will Grandpa have changed now he's retarded?'

One of the quickest ways to get a child's attention is to sit down and put your feet up.

Mothers work from 'Son up' to 'Sun down'.

Top marks for honesty to Wendy who wrote in a school essay: 'All our family has got a bad temper, with the exception of the cat.'

Youth is a time of rapid change. While your child is between the ages of 12 and 18 a parent can age 30 years.

Cleaning a home while the children are still growing is like shovelling the driveway before it stops snowing.

An American father once took his family on an educational trip to the West of America. The children were encouraged to record their impressions in a diary. One of the places they visited was the Grand Canyon, that incredible gorge, a mile deep, ten miles across and hundreds of miles long. That night after the children had gone to bed he studied the entries in their diary. His nine-year-old had written, 'Today I spat a mile.'

On the wall of the former Clashmore country school there hung a reproduction painting of the famous Venus de Milo sculpture. The visiting music teacher, noticing that one of the boys was biting his nails, said to him, 'Look at that picture and tell me what happens to people who bite their nails?' 'Please sir, they lose all their clothes.'

If children grew up according to early indications, we should have nothing but geniuses.

A small boy is someone who can wash his hands without getting the soap wet.

A city school teacher tells of once taking a pet rabbit to school to show her pupils. They were delighted and asked all kinds of questions. Finally one asked if it was a boy rabbit or a girl rabbit. At this the young teacher became slightly flustered. Finally she admitted she did not know. Then one little girl said, 'Please Miss, we could take a vote on it.'

A wee lad on the way back from nursery surprised his mother by saying, 'I am so glad you called me John.' When his mother asked why, he said, 'Because all the boys and girls at nursery call me John.'

A father was trying to encourage his dejected son by saying, 'Don't ever give up! People who are remembered never gave up. Think of Robert the Bruce, Madame Curie, Thomas Edison. They didn't give up. And look at Jonathan MacPringle.' The boy looked puzzled. 'Who's Johnathan MacPringle?' 'See,' said his father, 'you never heard of him. He gave up.'

Parental advice:

– To stay out of debt, act your wage.
– Too much make-up can be counter-seductive.
– The end does not always justify the jeans.
– Nothing is so humiliating as tripping over your own feat
– Drinking and driving can cause liquor mortis to set in.

Holy, Holy, Holy

A newspaper once offered a prize for the best brief answer to the question, 'What is wrong with the Church?' A Welsh minister won it with the following answer. 'What is wrong with the Church,' he said, 'is that it dwells too much upon what is wrong with it and overlooks its own wonder and destiny.'

As far back as I can remember, the church has been an integral part of my life. Each Sunday we worshipped together as a family. One of my earliest memories is of snuggling into my mother's fur coat during the service. There I felt very secure. Though I then had little understanding of what was being said, I believe the experience of worship was filling a God-shaped vacuum in my life, and was shaping my thinking and outlook. It was the church that nurtured in me an awareness of the eternal dimension to life, and a sense of the sacred. Later it was in the church youth organisations that I learned to speak in public, to sing (!) and act.

Despite all her warts, sores and blemishes, I love the church. I believe that without her the present darkness in the world would be remembered as a light to be coveted. In an article which Bernard Shaw once wrote for the *St Martins Review*, he said that if people ever found themselves deprived of churches, they would find they had been deprived of a necessity of life, which somehow has to be supplied. He thought the end result would probably be fuller churches.

The Church of St Paul, St Francis, John Wesley, Martin Luther King and Mother Teresa, and many other anonymous saints, has enriched the life of the world. The Church has kept on championing values that are too often neglected. To those tempted to spend their days in the 'thick of thin things', the church keeps speaking of ultimate concerns – birth and death, union and separation, faith, hope and love. Worship services remind us of what is of real worth.

My life would be much the poorer without the church.

During the Second World War, an Orkney minister had been asked to make a pulpit intimation about the formation in the congregation of a darning circle, to repair the socks of servicemen. It so happened this was the last intimation before he announced the opening hymn, *Holy, Holy, Holy*!

Pride is a deadly sin. It creates many problems in the church. But so too can taking a back seat. Most churches fill up from back to front. Often those who occupy the back seats complain that they have difficulty hearing the minister, and that they did not hear a word of what the little girl said, the one who read the lesson. Various solutions have been proposed as to how to get them to move forward:

– a heating system that does not reach the back rows.

– prizes randomly distributed in the front pews.

– installing a moving aisle to whisk down to the front those who arrive early.

– roping off the last four rows with a sign that reads, 'For mothers with noisy children'.

– announcing that the back pews are 'reserved for lost souls'.

An American minister once told of a man called Zeke who was a close friend of Adlai Stevenson. Zeke was much sought after for his advice on all kinds of problems. Once when asked why so many people came to him for advice, Zeke replied, 'Because I have got good judgment.' When then asked how he acquired such good judgment, he replied, 'It's the result of experience, and experience is the result of bad judgment!'

The Rev James Martin tells how he sent an assistant to call on an elderly man who had come to live with his daughter and husband. To the assistant's surprise it was the old man and not the daughter who answered the door. His daughter had been confined to bed by the doctor. The assistant minister accepted the old man's invitation to go through to his daughter's bedroom and see her. Shaking her warmly by the hand, he said, 'What on earth have you been doing to get yourself into this condition?' Learning subsequently that she was three months pregnant, he felt his opening words could have been better chosen!

A church magazine intimated that their Young Women's Group was having a Victorian evening. The hope was expressed that it would be a fun night, and 'that some of the women will wear clothes'!

In an article about a cookery book which was published as a fundraising effort by New Cathcart Church in Glasgow, the hope was expressed that the book might help ensure that the Kirk's 'coffins' were never empty.

Some ministers see their congregations nod approval while they sleep. In fact the church has been defined as 'a place where we encounter nodding acquaintances.' 'I know the man well,' said one member about another, 'we sleep in the same pew.'

An old Irishman who heard a minister read his sermon said, 'Glory be to God, if he can't remember it, how does he expect us to?'

Mary Carter tells how her grandfather was an ardent lay preacher. It worried him that he seemed to spend most of his time preaching to the converted. When one day a deacon told him at the close of the service that somebody had taken his new raincoat from the vestibule of the church, his eyes lit up: 'The Lord be praised. We're getting the sinners in at last.'

A minister remembers conducting a service in a crematorium. He said in his prayer, 'We thank you O God that Jesus still has the power to bring Lazarus from the grave to new life.' At this point the deceased's brother who was sitting at the front, said quietly but firmly, 'His name was Willie, not Lazarus.'

As a member of any church committee will tell you, after all is said and done, there is a lot more said than done.

During an ecumenical gathering, somebody rushed in and shouted, 'The building's on fire!' The Methodists gathered in a corner and prayed; the Baptists cried, 'Where's the water?'; the Christian Scientists agreed among themselves that there was no fire; the Fundamentalists shouted, 'It's the vengeance of God'; the Quakers quietly praised God for the blessings that fire brings; the Jews posted symbols on the doors, hoping the fire would pass; the Catholics passed the collection plate; the Episcopalians formed a procession and marched out in grand style; the Congregationalists shouted, 'Every man for himself.' And the Presbyterians? They appointed a chairperson who was to appoint a committee to look into the matter!

A Presbyterian minister in America, who had a Roman Catholic in his office staff, tells how shortly after she had been appointed, she had to type out the Apostle's Creed for the Church bulletin. Her ecumenical outlook prompted her to alter one of the clauses, so that it read, 'I believe in the Holy Presbyterian Church'.

Sermon titling can be a mixed blessing. One typesetter omitted the first 't' in immortality, so that the sermon read, 'I believe in immorality.'

Momentary dismay laid hold of the Rev Garner when he found his Sunday sermon title billed as 'CRUCIFICTION'.

The Rev Alec MacAlpine of Tain tells of reading a bible story to his three-year-old son, shortly after the birth of his little sister Annette. It was the story of Jesus calling the disciples. 'Jesus was walking by the sea of Galilee when he saw two brothers, Simon and his brother Andrew...' Andrew's face registered great joy when he heard that one of the fishermen had his name, but the smile quickly disappeared as his father read on, '...They were casting a net into the lake.' In a worried voice he said, 'Daddy, why did they throw Annette into the lake?'

A minister in Erie, Pennsylvania, tells how his four-year-old son asked him one day if God made the sunshine for the flowers to grow. 'Yes,' said his father. 'Does he make the dirt they grow in?' 'Yes,' said his father. 'And does he make the rain too?' When his father again answered in the affirmative, the little boy asked, 'Daddy, does God let Jesus hold the hose?'

'I never heard a sermon from which I did not derive some good,' said a fine old man, 'but I have had a few near misses.'

I sometimes feel church services should have a five-minute coughie break!

While preaching in a little country church a minister received one of the greatest compliments of his ministry. One old man gripped him by the hand at the door and said, 'Didn't get my usual nap today.'

A more doubtful compliment was that received by a Scottish minister. 'I no longer listen to the radio service before coming to church. With all these good preachers on the radio, it just isn't fair to you.'

Preaching once on the text, 'Whatsoever a man soweth, that shall he also reap', the minister told of a con-man, Horatio Bottomley, who engaged in a number of dubious financial projects. At last he was arrested. A friend who visited Horatio in prison found him stitching mail-bags. 'I see you're sewing,' said the visitor. 'No,' said Bottomley, 'reaping.'

Sam Levenson once said, 'How wise are thy commandments Lord. Each of them applies to somebody I know.'

If you do a thing twice in the Church, it is liable to become a 'tradition'.

The Seven Last Words of the Church: 'We never did it that way before.'

The minister announced that a number of buttons had been found among the coins in recent collections. He then added that it was his hope that in future the members would rend their hearts and not their garments.

A famous preacher once said he believed in extemporaneous preaching, but not extemporaneous preparation. He was thinking of those preachers who are guilty of waiting for the Spirit to start the motor when they have failed to provide any fuel. I love the honesty of an old German pastor, Klaus Harms. Once when a young minister said to him, 'I never prepare my sermons. I know that God will give me the right words to speak when I enter the pulpit.' Dr Harms replied, 'I am seventy years old, and I have preached for fifty years, but I must confess that all that time, not on one single occasion has the Holy Spirit spoken to me in the pulpit. But he spoke to me often as I left the pulpit, and what he said was, "Klaus, you've been lazy".'

Samuel Selvaretnam of Sri Lanka was a joyous Christian, a modern St Francis. One night he was riding in a train. He put his small case on the luggage rack above his seat and settled down to sleep. Luggage racks being notoriously vulnerable to thieves, he would wake up every few minutes to check his case was still there. After a few hours of such fitful sleep, he wakened, looked up and the bag was gone. 'After that,' said Selvaretnam, 'what a beautiful, sound sleep I had all the way home.'

An American farmer was approached to see if he would give hospitality to some delegates to a religious convention. He had provided bedroom accommodation the previous year. Since then he had, however, moved to a smaller house. He told the person who phoned that he now had only one spare room with a single bed, but he then added, 'If the delegates are as narrow as last time, you can send me ten.'

A church official sent a e-mail to a mission station which he was due to visit – 'Arriving Monday night'. When he finally did arrive, the man in charge looked at him with a bemused expression. 'I didn't know quite what to expect. Your e-mail read: Arriving Monday tight!'

A priest remembers the time his grocer searched his stock-room for a case of communion wine and inadvertently upset a box of household cleaner. Luckily it just missed the priest. 'Thank goodness,' said the grocer. Then with a glint in his eye, he added, 'I might have been had up for a bleach of the priest.'

A lady greeting her minister after the church service said, 'Your sermon this morning on telling the truth was... was... awful.'

Outlining at length the stiff nature of the final theology examination, the professor concluded his remarks by asking if anyone had any questions regarding the exam. The students sat in stunned silence. Finally one brave soul asked, 'Do you accept bribes?'

Another divinity student, in answer to one of the questions in the examination paper, drew a tombstone. It bore the words, 'Sacred to the memory which leaves me on occasions like this.'

Edward Kennedy told of a lecturer at a theological college who informed his class that the subject of his next lecture would be the sin of deceit and that, by way of preparation, he wished them all to read the seventeenth chapter of St Mark's Gospel. When the time came, he asked how many had complied with his instructions. Most of them raised their hands. 'Thank you,' said the lecturer, 'it is to people like you that today's lecture is especially addressed. There is no seventeenth chapter in Mark's Gospel.'

Mark Twain occasionally attended the services of Dr Doane, who later became Bishop of Albany. One Sunday morning, Twain said to him at the end of the service, 'I enjoyed your service this morning. I welcomed it like an old friend. I have a book at home that contains every word of it.' 'You have not,' said Dr Doane indignantly. The following day Mark Twain handed in to Dr Doane's home an unabridged dictionary.

A Presbyterian who turned Episcopalian on his death-bed, was asked why by his shocked relatives. 'I decided I wanted to be in a church where the bishops were visible.'

William Jennings Bryant stood unsuccessfully for President of the United States. Later he stood for Moderator of the General Assembly of the Presbyterian Church. He said he never really knew what politics was until he stood for Moderator!

On returning from a trip to the Far East, Philip Brooks the distinguished Boston minister, who wrote the carol *O Little Town of Bethlehem*, was asked by a friend what articles he had brought back with him and what customs duty he had to pay. The friend then jokingly asked if he had brought back a new religion from the Far East. Brooks replied that he had not, but then added with a glint in his eye, that if he had wanted to, there would have been no difficulty about customs duties, for America would be glad to import a religion without duties!

A vicar tells how as a bachelor he preached a sermon entitled, 'Rules for raising children.' After he got married and had children, he revised the sermon title for his new congregation to: 'Suggestions for raising children.' When his children got to be teenagers, he stopped preaching on that subject.

Two ladies in the congregation were always at one another's throats. Neither had a good word to say for the other. Come Saturday as Brigid was going into the Chapel, she met Maureen coming out. 'I've just been to confession,' said Maureen, glaring at her arch-enemy, 'but just you wait. Please God I won't always be in a state of grace.'

Once, when the habit of students shuffling their feet towards the end of a lecture particularly annoyed him, Prof A C Taylor looked up and said, 'Just allow me to cast one more pearl.'

Two ladies dressed in their new Easter rig-outs were having difficulty on Easter Sunday finding a seat in the church. Finally one said rather impatiently, 'Wouldn't you think that those people who do nothing but go to church Sunday after Sunday would stay home on Easter and leave room for the rest of us.'

A student once mentioned to a famous Scottish preacher that he had found the atmosphere in a certain kirk to be 'rather cold'. 'Cold,' cried the old man, 'Cold? I preached there two years ago and I haven't got the chill out of my bones yet.'

A priest once complained that a colleague had brought a surge of popularity to the ritual of confession. The first priest said he sometimes waited for an hour for someone to come to confess, but penitents formed long queues to tell all to the other priest. The explanation? The second priest was deaf.

A minister left instructions for the following epitaph to be inscribed on his tombstone:

> Go tell the church that I am dead
> But they need shed no tears.
> For though I'm dead, I'm no more dead
> Than they have been for years.

Of a learned and very liberal bishop it was said: 'He would believe anything provided it was not in Holy Scripture.'

Poor preaching has been defined as 'the expression of a two-minute idea with a half-hour vocabulary.'

'The church has gone to the dogs many times, but it is the dogs who have died each time.' G K Chesterton.

Dr Parkes Cadman once asked a divinity student who was a guest in his house to give thanks for the meal. The young man launched into a long prayer. Before the prayer was finished, Cadman broke in, 'That's all right Harry, the Lord knows now we're grateful. Let's eat.'

A newspaper report: 'Rev Macdonald presided, and opened and opened and opened the meeting with prayer.'

A minister who had occasion to preach on tact, proceeded thus: 'Tact is a praiseworthy thing. But as some o' ye may not rightly understand the meaning o' the word, I'll just give ye an illustration. Suppose for example one o' ye died an' went up tae the Gates o' Heaven. An' suppose ye met St Peter there, ye wouldna be sayin' onything tae him aboot cock-crowing. Weel, that's tact.'

On one of his visits to England, William James wrote a letter to *The Times*, which was not accepted for publication. It concerned a proposed Day of National Prayer, to which some people vociferously objected. They reminded him, James wrote, of a settler in Montana who suddenly came face-to-face with an enormous grizzly. He dropped to his knees and prayed, 'O Lord, I ain't never yet asked ye for help, and I ain't going to ask for none now, but for pity's sake, Lord, don't help the bear!'

H G Wells said of an ambitious young minister, 'He thought of gaiters, though he talked of wings.'

The Duke of Cambridge, George IV's younger brother, had a habit of making his own responses during church services. Once when the clergyman said, 'Let us pray', he was heard to say in a very audible voice, 'By all means.' On another occasion, when a clergyman prayed for rain, the Duke responded, 'No good so long as the wind is in the East.'

At the 1990 General Assembly of the Church of Scotland, Dr Finlay Macdonald intimated that the Business Committee had been approached to see if some ministers might volunteer to take part in a scientific experiment being carried out into 'stress' in various professions. The simplest test involved measuring the tremor of their fingertips. Dr Macdonald then informed the delegates that the scientist conducting the experiment was located in the entry hall of the nearby building owned by the Society of Friends, where Assembly lunches were being served. 'Perhaps in this instance,' he added, 'it might be more appropriate if I called the hall by its other name, the "Quaker" hall.'

An extreme instance of tongue-twistedness is said to have happened on Easter Sunday when the church was crowded to overflowing. Finding a lady somewhat disconcerted at being unable to occupy her usual place, the usher said, 'Madam, this pie is occupewd. May I sew you to another sheet?'

Ministers can also make some embarrassing mistakes. Bishop Fulton Sheen tells how he once met a man by the name of Lummock. His secretary helpfully pointed out that his name rhymed with stomach. The next day when he met the man, Bishop Sheen called him 'Kelly'.

Gerald Priestland tells how once during a radio discussion about religious language, he said unthinkingly (and later to his horror), 'the blood of Christ is not really my cup of tea.'

A Scottish minister who was waxing eloquent said, 'Remember that the same Creator who made the vast oceans, made the dewdrop; the Creator who made the mountains made the pebble; yes, and the same Creator who made me, made a daisy.'

A former Dean of Westminster, The Very Rev A C Don, said that when he was chaplain to the Commons, he went into the House every day, looked round at the members present, and then prayed for the country!

One Sunday, shortly before leaving Greenbank Church in Glasgow, where I had been assistant for two years, the minister asked me to wait in the vestry while he went into church and made the intimations. I was later embarrassed when I discovered he had been intimating to the congregation how they could contribute to my presentation. My embarrassment was caused by the fact that the theme of my children's address that morning was, 'It is more blessed to give than to receive.'

An Irish bishop tells how some people get nervous when they think they have to call him 'My Lord', especially the nuns. On one occasion as one of them was serving him a cup of coffee, she picked up the sugar bowl and said, 'How many lords, my lump?'

A Sunday school teacher was telling her class about the birth of Jesus. When she came to that part about there being no room at the inn, one boy said, 'Please Miss, I blame Joseph. He should have booked.'

One little boy was concerned to know who the fourth person was in the bed at Bethlehem. He thought the carol said, 'Away in a manger, no crib, four in a bed.' Even the Biblical story, if not punctuated carefully, can give the impression of a crowded manger. 'Mary and Joseph and the babe lying in the manger.' A little Glasgow lad was heard to sing, 'A wean in a manger' (wean, pronounced 'wain', is the Glasgow word for baby or young child).

After one of the kings had presented the gold to the baby Jesus, and before the third presented the myrrh, the second young king came forward with his present. He said to Mary and Joseph, 'Frank sent it.'

A woman remarked to her friend that for Christmas she had got a visit from a jolly bearded fellow with a great big bag over his shoulder. 'My son came home from university with his laundry!'

General Eva Burrows, the leader of the Salvation Army, tells of a nativity play which was put on when she was a teacher in a small mission station in Zimbabwe. There were eight angels. Six were black, but two were blonde, the daughters of a Norwegian couple who worked at the mission station. During the dress rehearsals Eva was standing at the back of the stage directing the angels, in their tinselled haloes, white robes and wings. During a pause in the rehearsals, Eva Burrows heard one of the Norwegian girls saying to the other, 'Do you think there will be black angels in heaven?' 'Of course there will,' replied her sister. 'Anyhow, Jesus would not know the difference.'

The school chaplain reminded the infant classes who had been excitedly telling him about their hoped for presents, that Christmas is a time for giving and sharing, not just receiving. His remarks clearly had an effect, for when one of the teachers emptied the class letter-box at the end of the afternoon, she found the following note: 'Dear Father Christmas, I will share all my toys. Please can I have lots to share.'

Rebuking her small son for not going to church willingly, his mother said, 'You go to the pictures for entertainment, and you go over to Freddie's house and over to Tommy's house, and you have a nice time. Now don't you think it's only right that once a week you should go to God's house, just for one hour?' The boy thought it over and then said, 'But Mum, what would you think if you were invited to somebody's house and every time you went, the fellow wasn't there?'

Advent is the religious equivalent of the secular message that there are only twenty-four shopping days to Christmas.

Lent is when people give up such things as sweets and cakes, thus ridding themselves of the sin of gluttony, only to boast about their achievements and commit the sin of pride.

When a Bible Class teacher asked her class why the Puritans went to America, one youngster replied, 'To have freedom to worship in their own way – and make other people worship in the same way.'

When Princess Marina was a little girl, she lived with her parents and sisters and English governess in Athens. She had a set bedtime each night. Like many children, she often tried to put it off. One night her excuse was rather unique. She said to her governess, 'Foxy, lots of other girls are going to bed now. God must be very busy listening to their prayers. If I go to bed later on, the rush will be over, and God will have more time to listen to me.'

The Bishop of Bath and Wells tells of a religious instruction teacher who took some primary children out into the woods one day to share with them something of the wonder of God's world. The children had a lovely time following nature trails and listening to the birds. Towards the end of the day she said to the children, 'Let us thank God for what we have seen and done in the open air.' She then asked the children if there were any things they would specially like to thank God for. She was soon to regret asking this question, for one little boy said, 'Thank you God for such a lovely tree to wee-wee behind.'

The minister was doing a series of children's talks based on everyday things. One week he held up a packet of salt and asked the children, 'What does salt do?' The reply was not what he expected. 'It gives you high blood pressure.'

A teacher wanting to explore the notion of God that young children had, began by asking them, 'Who is God?' There was silence, but finally one six-year-old boy said, 'God is the man who saved the Queen.'

When the teacher asked, 'How long do you think Adam and Eve were in the garden before being expelled?' one boy surprised her by saying, 'At least until September.' When asked what made him think that, he said, 'That is when apples are ripe.'

When a minister asked the children why coffee was served in the hall at the close of the service, one boy said, 'To get people wide awake before they drive home.'

Jack Webster tells of a Buchan teacher who was giving a lesson on children's pets. To her surprise one boy announced that his dog was called 'Moreover'. When she expressed doubt about such a name, the little chap assured her of his authority: 'Miss, it says in the Bible, "Moreover the dog came and licked his sores".'

A new Anglican minister had come to town. His clerical dress was not unlike that of a Roman Catholic priest. One day he chanced to pass several little catholic boys in the street. One of them shouted, 'Good morning, Father.' No sooner had he passed than he heard one of the boys turn on his friend in disgust. 'Father! He's no father, he's got three kids.'

Addressing a gathering of schoolboys, a bishop gave this example of moral courage: 'A boy in a dormitory who, in front of all the others, kneels down and says his prayers before hopping into bed.' He then asked the boys if they could think of another example. 'Sir,' piped up one voice, 'a minister in a dormitory full of ministers, hopping into bed *without* saying his prayers.'

Raising the Rafters

A friend who was minister in one of the large housing areas of Glasgow, tells how he once visited a home where the young husband had died tragically. The house being in a very poor state, Bob suggested that the funeral might be from his church, stressing that there would be no charge. The woman readily accepted his offer. Unaware that she had never had any connection with the church, he then inquired what hymn she would like at the service. When she admitted she did not know any hymns, he suggested they might have the 23rd Psalm. On hearing this her eyes lit up. 'That would be wonderful,' she said. 'My husband's birthday was on the 23rd.'

Not to have any knowledge of the *Shepherd Psalm*, or the other great hymns of the church, that would be a great loss. I am glad I learned many of the great hymns of faith at an early age. I sometimes wonder if my father, who was a church organist, ever really forgave me for going to the pulpit instead of the organ! But I am certainly grateful that he introduced me to the wonderful world of church music. Often when walking or driving I find myself humming a favourite hymn. In times of setback or disappointment or bereavement, a verse of a hymn has often given me '*strength for today, and bright hope for tomorrow.*'

For me there are few experiences more uplifting or exciting than singing hymns in a packed kirk. The popularity of such radio and television programmes as *Songs of Praise* and *Sunday Half-Hour* would seem to indicate that I am by no means alone in my love of hymn-singing. For many viewers and listeners, warm memories cluster round familiar hymns.

It is not surprising that hymn singing should be such an integral part of Christian worship, for the Christian faith is too joyful a thing for the cold prose of ordinary speech.

> Crumble, crumble, voiceless things
> No faith can last that never sings.

The church's attitude ought to be more a 'hip-hip-hooray' attitude than a 'no-no' one. There is no doubt that the greatest days of the Church have been its singing days.

A church organist was determined to break the congregation's habit of talking during the opening voluntary. The prelude he selected started quietly, but ended with every stop in the organ pulled out. Two elderly women who were chatting before the voluntary, kept on talking, raising their voices louder and louder to overcome the organ's increasing volume. What they did not know, but of course the organist knew, was the abruptness of the ending of the voluntary. It caught one of the women in mid-sentence. All sounds suddenly became silence, pierced by the immortal words: 'My John likes his fried.'

Pipe organs are often more than one organ. Some are two, some three, some five, depending on the generosity of the donor. Dornoch Cathedral is a two manual organ – a great organ and a swell organ. In saying that, I am not boasting – it is just the way organs are named. 'Swell' means the one on top, 'Great' the one below.

Unfortunately not all church members realise this. The Rev Paul Corcoran tells of a church committee who were interviewing candidates for the post of organist. One candidate, a lady, said, 'I see you have a swell organ.' 'Thank you,' said one of the committee, 'we think it's nice too.' The candidate withdrew her application!

The Drumchapel organist was puzzled by a note he received from a bride, asking if he would play *Annie Maria* at her wedding! Did she mean *Annie Laurie* or *Ave Maria*?

When someone sings his own praise, he usually gets the tune too high.

One lady gushed to the handsome young organist at the end of the service, 'I just love to hear you impoverish at the organ.' In some churches that might be too near the truth to be funny. Organ improvisations can sometimes leave much to be desired.

An old lady who had no relish for new hymns, expressed her strong dislike of the new Hymn Book. 'But,' said her friend, 'David sang new hymns to Saul.' 'Well I now understand,' she said, 'why Saul finally threw his javelin at David.'

> To our objective point of view
> No hymn is lovely if it is new.

James Henderson, the Editor of the *Northern Times*, recalls attending a sub-editing course. One exercise was to condense and headline a minister's letter bemoaning new trends in the church. In the letter the minister had expressed his concern about the trends towards wearing more casual clothes in church, and about the use of modern translations of the Bible and new hymns –

some sung to the accompaniment of the guitar instead of the organ. If these trends were not halted, he said, he could envisage the day coming when these awful modern hymns would be sung by semi-nude choristers. One young genius on the course proposed the following possible headline for the letter: 'Jazzed up hymns and topless hers.'

As part of Dornoch Cathedral's 750th celebrations, some of the members volunteered to make tapestry cushions for the choir stalls, cushions depicting local birds and wild flowers. When the first one was completed, a cushion depicting the owl, I showed it to the Church office-bearers. A sentence in the Minute of that meeting caused great hilarity: 'Mr Simpson showed the members of the Court the owl, which is to be placed alongside the other birds in the choir-stalls.' Fortunately the lady members of the choir who were present took it as a compliment.

Was Adam and Eve's favourite hymn 'A bite with me'?

In some Scottish homes the hymn 'Let us with a gladsome mind, praise the Lord for he is kind', was sung as a grace before meals. A Dr Caldwell told me how as a boy, he thought grown-ups were singing, 'Let us with a glass of wine, praise the Lord...'

A Yorkshire paper in its 'Hundred Years Ago' column recalled how at a Methodist Chapel, an elderly worshipper in poor circumstances and with the soles of his shoes worn through, frequently called out during the sermon to give vent to his religious fervour. He'd say things like 'Hallelujah!' 'Praise the Lord!' 'The Lord be with us!' but his interjections so irritated a prosperous and more restrained churchgoer in the next pew that he said he'd buy him some new boots if the old man kept quiet during the next three meetings. The old boy, who was known as 'Hallelujah Tom', kept quiet for two of them, but at the third meeting his feelings got the better of him, and he jumped up shouting, 'Boots or no boots – Hallelujah! Hallelujah! Hallelujah!'

C A Joyce tells of a new army recruit whose number was 254. The soldier wrote to his mother, 'Last Sunday I went to church for the first time. Suddenly a man in a white shirt got up and said, "Number 254, art thou weary? Art thou languid?" and I stood up and said, "Yes sir, I'm exhausted." Well the sergeant put me in the cells.'

A father used to sing hymns to his children to send them to sleep until one night he overheard his four-year-old son whisper to his younger sister, 'If you pretend you're asleep, he'll stop.'

For many years Charles Warr and Harry Whitley were associate ministers at St Giles in Edinburgh. Having different concepts of the ministry and the role of St Giles, there was considerable tension between the two men. At one stage it was rumoured that on those Sundays when Whitley conducted worship, he always included the Paraphrase that prayed for the day when '*war* would be no more'.

Dr Luccock once said to a congregation who had just finished lustily singing *Onward Christian Soldiers*, 'You sang, *Like a mighty army, Moves the church of God.*
'Now just suppose the army accepted the lame excuses that many people think are good enough to serve as an alibi for not attending Church.

'Imagine this. Reveille 7 am. Squad on the parade ground. The sergeant barks out, "Count fours. One! Two! Three! Number Four missing. Where is Private Smith?"

'"Smith was too sleepy to get up this morning sergeant," pipes up one soldier. "He was out late last night and needed the sleep. He said to tell you that he would be with you in spirit."

'"That's fine," said the sergeant, "Remember me to him."

'"Where's Brown?" asks the sergeant.

'"Oh he's out playing golf," said the other chap. "He only gets one day a week for recreation, and you know how important that is."

'"Sure sure," the sergeant replies cheerfully. "Hope he has a good game. Where's Robinson?"

'"Robinson," explains a buddy, "is entertaining guests today and of course couldn't come. Besides he was at drill last week."

'"Fine," said the sergeant. "Tell him he is welcome any time he is able to drop in."

'Can you imagine any conversation like that ever happening in the army? Such soldiers would get twenty days in the guard-house. Yet how often you hear such remarks in church, said with a straight face. Like a mighty army! Why if the church really moved like an army, many of her members would have to be court-martialled.'

A minister once referred to his choir as 'the war-department of the Church.'

Sarah Rutty of the BBC tells how the *Daily Service* on Radio 4 was transmitted live from St Peter's, a dimly lit church in Vere Street in London. The rehearsal had gone fine, but just as the red light flashed on, there was a loud rustling noise in one of the pews. The BBC singers watched helplessly as a dishevelled and irate tramp emerged shaking his makeshift paper and cardboard bed in all directions, at the same time giving vent in colourful fashion to his fury at having been so rudely wakened by the hymn singing. There was however nothing they could do. As the commissionaire hurried him through the door, the presenter opened with the words, 'Good morning and welcome to our daily service. Our theme today is the Peace of God.'

> 'Swans sing before they die – 'twere no bad thing
> Did certain persons die before they sing.'
>
> Coleridge

Every hymn-book categorises hymns for special occasions. The following might be appropriate hymns for special groups of people:

Card users: – 'A charge to keep I have'.
Investors: – 'And can it be that I should gain'.
Prisoners: – 'Yield not to temptation'.
Politicians: – 'Standing on the promises'.
Courting couples: – 'Sometimes a light surprises'.
Chain smokers: – 'I need thee every hour'.
Prisoners: – 'Fling wide the gates'.
Lawyers: – 'Come my soul thy suit prepare'.
Launderers: – 'Oh for a faith that will not shrink'.
Corsetieres: – 'All is safely gathered in'.
Dog lovers: – 'O master let me walk with thee'.
Cyclists: – 'Ride on, Ride on'.
Fishermen: – 'We shall gather at the river'.

A Mrs Rawstorne, who worshipped with us from time to time, was the grand-daughter of the famous hymn-writer Sabine Baring-Gould. She told how at the time of her wedding her mother expressed her disappointment that she was unwilling to have one of her grandfather's hymns included in the wedding service. 'But mother,' she finally said, 'which one would you choose as being suitable for a wedding – *The Day of Resurrection*; *Through the Night of Doubt and Sorrow*; *Onward Christian Soldiers*, *Marching as to War*, or *Now the Day is Over, Night is Drawing Nigh*?'

A church had planned a service using the talents of its young people. One teenage girl had been asked to play the piano during the uplifting of the offering. No one had enquired, however, what she was going to play. A smile appeared on the face of the treasurer as he recognised the theme from the film *The Sting*, for he suspected that was how some of the members regarded the offering.

An American doctor, Peter Mackay, told me the hymns he most disliked were the 7/11 ones. When I asked him what he meant, he replied, 'Those modern hymns with seven words sung eleven times!'

A Salvation Army officer tells how a picture appeared in the local paper showing their band playing hymns in the town centre. In the photograph, next to where the band had been playing there was a large placard outside a shop. The placard, which the members of the brass band had not noticed, read: 'Ear Piercing'.

Harriet, a member of the local church choir, used to enjoy relaxing at the end of the day by singing hymns in her bath. After one rather lengthy session of singing negro spirituals, the doorbell rang. When she finally got there, she found a note which had been pushed through the letter-box by one of her neighbours in the flat. The note read, 'Sing low, sweet Harriet'.

So highly reverenced was the Psalter in the 19th-century church that there was an aversion to using the actual words of the Psalms for choir practices. Secular words were used instead. Many of these alternative verses revealed a pawky sense of humour:

O mither dear, John Lawrie's lum
When shall it sweepit be?
For a' the soot's come doon the lum
And spoilt my granny's tea.

I wish I were a brewer's horse
Three quarters of the year
I'd turn my head where tail should be
And drink up all the beer.

(The brewer's horse often had as much beer in its stomach as on its back, since it was fed the unsold stock.)

The furore caused by the introduction of the organ and hymns into the Scottish Kirk is well known. Not so well known are the rows caused by the introduction of the pitch-fork to help precentors. 'See what things are coming to,' cried an old lady when she saw her precentor using a pitch-fork for the first time. 'See what he's doin', actually usin' cauld steel in the service o' God!'

Parsons and Persons

I have no regrets about leaving the world of science and becoming a minister. A minister is privileged to spend a large part of his time doing what other people can only do part time – being a friend to many. He is also privileged to get close to people when life is most real to them; when a baby is born, when a young couple decide to live the rest of their lives together, when a person dies. To be able to shed light on the mystery of life, to be supportive of those wrestling with problems they cannot solve, but must learn to live with, there is no more satisfying job in the world.

An eighteenth-century church publication carried the following dire warning. 'If any person or persons shall be guilty of speaking against the minister, or of speaking against his preaching, the said person or persons shall be punished by fine or whipping.'

How the pendulum has swung. Today, few professions are criticised or parodied as much as the Christian ministry. If his sermon is slightly longer than usual, 'He puts people to sleep.' If it is shorter, 'He has not bothered preparing.' If he is young, he lacks experience. If he is old, he ought to retire. Though a few ministers may give the impression of being more religious than God, and speak as though they had a cathedral in their mouths, they are the exception. As in other professions the minority have given the majority a bad press.

At public functions some treat you as a normal human being who is interested in normal everyday things. A few challenge you about what the church teaches. But others treat you with a condescending deference, as one might treat a well meaning but rather drab maiden aunt who would never say boo to a goose, who is not, they suspect, subject to the normal feelings and temptations that beset most other people. I know which of the attitudes I prefer. I much prefer being treated as a man rather than an angelic softie who belongs to a kind of third sex. Had the early church been made up of such anaemic pastors, it would never have made it into the second century.

Parson is old English for Person. There may be a few phonies and Holy Willies in the ministry, but the majority I have found to be genuine persons, kindly, caring men and women, with not only a deep love for God, but also a great love of life and healthy fun. I enjoy their company.

The Rev John Connor said, 'In all my ministry I have set up, taken down, arranged and rearranged so many chairs, that I am well conditioned to accept the fact that being a "chairperson" represents more *toil* than title.'

Ministers have always had a sense of humour, but unfortunately some in the past have felt that the feeling of awe in which they were then held, made it necessary that this quality should not have undue prominence. The strength of this feeling of awe in certain parts of Scotland, is illustrated by the story of the mother who was walking along the street in a West Highland village when suddenly she gave her young son a dig in the ribs. 'Straighten your cap, George,' she said. 'Here comes the minister's dog.'

A former Moderator of the Church of Scotland, Dr Archie Craig, loved to tell how on a train journey, a lady seated opposite, noted that he was reading a theological book, but was not wearing a dog collar. She asked why.

'I'm an ordained minister,' he replied, 'but I'm not now in the parish.'

The lady nodded her head kindly and asked, 'Was it drink?' Dr Craig was at that time Secretary of the British Council of Churches!

Happy is the minister with a wife to tell him what to do, and an assistant to do it.

An American minister who exchanged pulpits with the Free Church minister in Golspie, was welcomed on his arrival in Sutherland by two of the church officials, Hugh and Sandy Gunn. With a mischievous glint in his eye, the American commented on the uniqueness of the welcome. Never before, he said, had he been met by a 'Double-barrelled gun!' One of the Gunns replied, with a twinkle in his eye, 'Aye, but at least you'll never be met by a canon in the Free Kirk.'

Thomas Macaulay, the statesman and writer was a compulsive talker. After his return from India, the Rev Sydney Smith professed to notice an improvement. 'His enemies might have said before that he talked rather too much, but now he has occasional flashes of silence, that make his conversation delightful.'

A Glasgow minister who was a pipe smoker recalled an assistant who was not only a compulsive talker but also a heavy smoker. Concerned about the number of cigarettes he was smoking, the assistant decided to switch to a pipe. Shortly after making this change, they spent some time discussing church business. As usual the assistant talked a great deal. By the time he left there was a great pile of matches in the ashtray. 'My pipe doesn't seem to work as well as yours,' he said. As graciously as he could, Dr Stewart hinted that perhaps his pipe might work better if he spoke less and listened more.

During the week of prayer for Christian unity, at a service in one of Belfast's more ecumenically minded Presbyterian churches, Father James Quinn, the distinguished Jesuit priest, was given the opportunity of bringing greetings from the Roman Church. With a smile on his face, he began, 'Friends, non-Romans, countrymen.'

An Assembly Moderator who was urging commissioners to move along in their deliberations, commented, 'Everything needs to be said, but it doesn't need to be said by everybody.'

Dr George Macleod, the distinguished founder of the Iona Community, was a controversial figure in the Scottish kirk. In the summer he employed young men, often divinity students, to shepherd round the ancient Iona sites the flocks of tourists who invaded the island. A student had just described to a small group the significance of *Relig Oran*, the ancient graveyard with its headstones of early Scottish and Norwegian kings, and still the resting place for islanders today. As he was about to move to the next point of interest (St Martin's Cross), a lady in the group asked rather plaintively, 'And where is Dr Macleod buried?' The student's reply gave Dr George considerable pleasure. 'Dr Macleod,' he replied, 'is not dead yet.' Then with a mischievous glint in his eye the student added, 'Unfortunately!'

During a tour which the tireless Dr Macleod made of America when he was ninety, several Americans were slightly put off by his constantly referring to 'Iona Community'. They thought he was boasting, 'I own a community.'

A biographer of Gilbert and Sullivan tells how once when W S Gilbert arrived at a provincial hotel to stay the night, he was alarmed to find it filled by clergymen attending a theological conference. He confessed to one of them, 'I feel like a lion in a den of Daniels.'

The language of some football supporters on the train left much to be desired. Finally one of them apologised to the minister who was in the compartment. 'We call a spade a spade,' he said. 'That surprises me,' said the minister, 'I would have thought you would have called it a b— shovel.'

The Rev James Martin tells of an assistant who announced, 'Next Sunday the Sacrament of the Lord's Supper will be dispensed with in this church.'

Dr Steimle's grandfather was a Lutheran minister in New York in the mid-nineteenth century. He was a well-known figure in the neighbourhood. He was also a soft touch for every pan-handler on the street. His wife, alarmed at the steady drain on their limited financial resources, determined to do something about it. She gathered up his loose change and put it into a little pouch, tied at the top, to carry in his pocket, thinking this would deter his giving to every beggar who came along. But she figured wrong. The first pan-handler who came up to him, got the whole pouch with the parting words, 'God must have meant you to have it all.'

A minister inquired of a parishioner, 'What do you have against the church?' 'Plenty,' he said. 'The first time I went they threw water on my face. The second time they tied me to a woman I've had to support ever since. The next time they'll throw dirt on me.'

Al Smith, when Governor of the State of New York, attended a winter weekend party at a friend's house in New Hampshire. On Sunday he got up with two Roman Catholics in the party at 5.30am to drive thirty miles to attend early Mass. It was freezing outside. As he put on his second sweater and then his coat, he turned and looked at his Protestant friends sleeping. He was heard to murmur as he stepped out into the cold, 'Wouldn't it be awful if it turned out they were right and we were wrong?'

Canon Streeter once told of two London cabbies who were watching a lordly figure descend the steps of a large mansion house. He glittered as he walked! The one cabbie turned to the other and said, 'Bill, did you ever hear of God? Well, that's Archibald his brother.'

Writing to a local sweet manufacturing company about the possibility of contributing something to the church sale, the minister ended his letter, 'Hoping for a flavourable reply.'

The Rev Bill Ritson tells how a photograph which was certainly not flattering, appeared once in the local paper. Because of the lighting, his clerical collar was virtually invisible. He consequently appeared to have an extra-ordinarily long white neck, rather like a goose. His eyes seemed to be popping out of his head as they stared at the camera in wild alarm through his big glasses. He was somewhat reassured when the following Sunday one of his members said to him, 'I saw your picture in the paper. You looked like the famous film star.' Momentarily he preened himself, wondering if she might mean Michael Caine or Robert Redford, until she said, 'You looked just like ET.'

Dr Norman Macleod, Queen Victoria's favourite Scottish minister, told how one day when on his way to the Barony Church in Glasgow, he saw two street urchins making a building out of mud. 'What are you making?' asked Dr Macleod. 'We're making a kirk, and there's the pulpit,' said the boys. 'But where's the minister?' 'We havenae enough dirt to mak a meenister,' was the crushing reply. Dr Macleod went off chuckling to himself.

Professor Karl Barth tells of a divinity student who had just arrived in Basle. Mistaking Barth for a university official, he inquired of him if he knew the world-famous theologian Karl Barth. Back came the quick reply: 'Know him! I shave him every morning.'

In the course of a conversation which Prime Minister Gladstone once had with the Archbishop of Canterbury, Gladstone said, 'I understand, your Grace, that you do not altogether approve of my dealing with the Irish question?' Back came the reply, 'It's not your dealing to which I object. It's your shuffling.'

Norman Vincent Peale told of an 86-year-old woman who was flying for the first time. Over the plane's intercom she heard the announcement: 'This is your captain speaking. Our number four engine has just been shut off because of mechanical trouble. However, there is nothing to worry about. We will continue our flight with three engines and will land on schedule. Also, I have some really assuring news for you. We have four Methodist bishops on board.' The elderly passenger, who had been listening apprehensively, called the stewardess. 'Would you please tell the captain that I would rather have four engines and three bishops.'

'There is a special place in heaven for the wives of clergymen,' remarked a parishioner to the vicar's wife. 'Oh,' replied the vicar's wife, 'I'd much rather stay with my husband.'

When an army padre one day saw, in the front-line trenches, an archbishop in gaiters and a tin hat, talking to the troops, he commented on the fact that though his legs were firmly rooted in the past, his head was at least moving with the times.

Dentist to minister patient: 'I realise how hard it is for you to open your mouth and not say anything, but please try.'

A minister who had bought a cheap second-hand car, later admitted how hard it was to drive a bargain! He called the car 'Flattery' because it got him nowhere. Finally he let it 'Rust in Peace'.

Another minister labelled the file for his bills, 'Due unto others'.

The Rev Leith Fisher said, 'I have always been suspicious of the turnip lantern as a visual aid ever since I took one into the pulpit and one of my elders said he wasn't sure who was the better looking.'

An article in the *Canadian Doctor* tells of the following series of advertisements which reputedly appeared in a newspaper.

Monday: 'The Reverend A J Jones has one television set for sale. Telephone 556 1234 after 7pm and ask for Mrs Smith who lives with him cheap.'

Tuesday: 'We regret any embarrassment to Reverend Jones caused by a typographical error in yesterday's paper. It should have read. "The Reverend A J Jones has one television set for sale cheap. Telephone 556 1234 and ask for Mrs Smith who lives with him after 7pm".'

Wednesday: 'Reverend Jones informs us that he has received several annoying telephone calls because of an incorrect advertisement in yesterday's paper. It should have read: "The Reverend Jones has one television set for sale cheap. Telephone 556 1234 after 7pm and ask for Mrs Smith who loves with him".'

Thursday: 'Please note that I, Reverend A J Jones, have no television set for sale. I have smashed it – don't ring 556 1234 any more. I have not been carrying on with Mrs Smith and until yesterday Mrs Smith was my housekeeper.'

Friday: 'Housekeeper wanted. Usual duties, good pay, love in. Contact Reverend A J Jones, Telephone 556 1234.'

Rabbi Lionel Blue told on the radio about a man for whom everything had been going wrong. His business had failed, his health was poor, his wife had gone. One morning at breakfast his buttered toast fell from the table and landed buttered side up. Wondering if his luck had changed, he went and told the rabbi about what had happened. Was this a sign that things were going to improve? The rabbi stroked his beard and said as rabbis often do, 'That is a difficult question. I will have to consult with my fellow-rabbis.' Finally, several days later, he came to see the man. 'I'm sorry but we have decided you made a terrible mistake. You buttered the wrong side of the bread.'

Bishop Fulton Sheen was once the guest speaker at a rally which was held in an American theatre. When a collection was announced, he inquired as to what the collection was for. The answer he received was, 'To hire better speakers next year.'

On another occasion when Bishop Sheen was speaking, a drunk in the gallery began heckling in an unintelligible manner. Finally the Bishop quietened him by saying, 'The only person who likes to be interrupted in the middle of a sentence is a prisoner.'

Douglas Horton tells how in the popular mind the leader of the progressive forces at the Second Vatican Council was Cardinal Bea, and the anchormen of the conservatives were the Curia. Now in the course of the Roman Mass the congregation said '*Mea* (I am) *culpa* (to blame)' and finally '*Mea* (I am) *maxima* (very greatly) *culpa* (to blame).' The story is told that when the Curia said these words, they murmured, '*Bea culpa ... Bea maxima culpa*'. At another point in the Mass comes '*Kyrie* (Lord) *eleison* (be merciful),' which Cardinal Bea is said to have recited as, '*Curia eleison*'.

An American priest, Father Taylor, once prayed, 'Lord we ask thee for a Governor who will rule in the fear of the Lord, who will defeat the ringleaders of corruption, enhance the prosperity of the State, promote the happiness of the people. O Lord, what's the use of beating about the bush. Give us George Briggs for Governor.'

Bishop Wilberforce used to tell of a clergyman who when asked to say grace would look to see if there were champagne glasses on the table. If there were he would begin, 'O most bountiful Jehovah...' but if he saw only claret glasses, he would pray, 'We are not worthy Lord of these the least of thy mercies.'

A clergyman who had been given a very flowery introduction began his after-dinner speech by saying, 'May the Lord forgive your chairman his excesses, and me for enjoying them so much.'

George Milham tells how their priest, who had suddenly become ill, had asked his twin brother, also a priest, to fill in for him and conduct a funeral service that day. His brother agreed. It was not until the priest was accompanying the coffin down the aisle, however, that he realised he had neglected to ask the sex of the deceased. This was information he would need for his remarks during the service. As he approached the relatives sitting in the front pew, he nodded towards the coffin and whispered to one woman, 'Brother or sister?' 'Cousin,' she replied.

For many years Dr Ronald Falconer was the head of BBC religious broadcasting in Scotland. Among the guests at his retiral dinner were three distinguished ministers of the church: Dr George Macleod, Dr William Barclay (described once by a Glasgow lady as that deaf old man who talks on television about the Bible), and John R Gray. In the chair that night was Alasdair Milne, the head of BBC. Dr Falconer recalls how at the beginning of the proceedings, Alasdair Milne muttered, as was his habit, into his plate, 'I am going to ask Lord Macleod [here he lifted his head and spoke to his right] to say Grace.' Everybody rose and George Macleod took a deep breath. Dr Barclay who had picked up only the last three words in his hearing aid, trolled out in characteristic tones, 'For what we are about to receive, may the Lord make us truly thankful.' As the company sat down, their laughter exploded, as John R Gray said, *sotto voce*, 'The voice was the voice of Jacob, not of Esau.'

When an outspoken young delegate to a conference chaired by the late Dr Fisher suggested that the Archbishop's generation were now back numbers, Dr Fisher politely replied, 'Maybe, but back numbers are useful for lighting fires.'

A minister had been preaching in a vacant charge for two Sundays in a row. He had come to recognise a certain short-sighted lady who came puffing up the brae with her Bible and hymn book under her arm. When he drew abreast of her, he stopped and offered her a lift which she gratefully accepted. At the church door he politely helped her out on to the pavement 'Who's preaching the day?' she enquired. Modestly he mentioned his own name. The old lady began to fumble at the car door in a sudden panic. 'Here,' she said, 'could ye just gie me a wee hurl hame.'

Though no longer a part of Sunday congregations, sheep dogs are still very much part of Highland life. During lambing season they will often finish the day exhausted, but not a single sheep will have been lost. A poetic Highland preacher once elaborated on this fact.

'The Lord is my shepherd. Aye and more than that, he has two collie dogs, named Goodness and Mercy. With the shepherd before, and them behind, even poor sinners like you and me can hope to win home at the last.'

The old shepherd was being reproached by the minister about his absence from his usual place in the Kirk. When the shepherd explained that he had been attending the church in the neighbouring parish, the minister said, 'I'm not happy about this running away to strange kirks. How would you like to see your sheep straying into strange pastures?' Back came the caustic reply, 'I wouldna gie a docken if it was better grass.'

Father Hughes was for many years the Roman Catholic chaplain to Glasgow University. He was respected by Protestant and Catholic students alike. He was a keen supporter of the ecumenical movement. His superior, Archbishop Scanlon, who had grave reservations about the existence and style of Father Hughes' ecumenical services, was suddenly taken ill and rushed to hospital. Shortly after being discharged, he decided to move Father Hughes from the University post to a parish appointment. One wit attributed the move to the Archbishop having had his 'Protestant gland' removed in hospital.

An Episcopal bishop's daughter had become friendly with a young man who was an agnostic. The first time she took him home, to her consternation her father asked him to say grace. In a low voice he muttered some unintelligible words. When the Amen had been spoken, the Bishop said, 'I am sorry, but I didn't understand a word you said.' Quick as a flash the young man replied, 'I wasn't talking to you.'

One Saturday evening the Dumbarton Presbytery Clerk had to contact a minister in the Presbytery. The minister's wife, who answered the phone, explained that her husband had just returned from a wedding reception, and had retired to bed to unwind. Knowing that the reception had been in a hotel renowned for its wine cellar, the clerk said he was tempted to ask the minister's wife if there was an 'e' in 'unwined'!

When the Rev Dr Drummond was ninety, he was persuaded by some friends to have his photograph taken. When the young photographer said he hoped he might have the honour of photographing him on his hundredth birthday, Dr Drummond replied, 'Well, I don't see why not. You look very healthy.'

A member of a church vacancy committee, who was perturbed at the decision of the other members of the committee to go for a very young minister, expressed his concern that their outlook was being too influenced by

a text from the parable of the Prodigal Son, 'Give me a
kid that I may make merry with my friends.'

> I never see my minister's eyes
> No matter how bright they shine
> When he prays he shuts them tight
> When he preaches he closes mine.
>
> If he can remember so many jokes
> With all the details that mould them
> Why can't he remember with equal skill
> How many times he told them?

Angus Mackenzie, the minister of Lochinver for
many years, learned to drive long before the days of
driving tests or published Highway Codes. He had his
own rules for driving on the one-track roads which are
so characteristic of the West Highlands. Angus loved to
tell of a new policeman who had been posted to
Lochinver. His most striking characteristic was his
constant use of big words. The problem was, they were
not always the right ones. The first time he and Angus
Mackenzie travelled together, the policeman was
horrified at the way Angus ignored many of the rules of
the road. Finally he asked Angus if he had ever read *The
Highway Code*. When Angus confessed he had not, the
policeman said, 'Well minister, I think you should get a
copy and pursue it incontinently.'

The Very Rev Dr Bill McDonald of Mayfield, in his
retiring address as Moderator, told how during a
Moderatorial visit to Dundee, he was presented in one
school with a book of essays by the primary children,
entitled, *What does the Moderator do all day?* It made
fascinating reading. 'After breakfast he goes round the
houses to make fiends. After lunch he will go and see

other Moderators. After tea he likes to relax by watching TV. For supper he has pancakes and tea and goes to bed.' Another read, 'After breakfast the Moderator goes out and walks to the Church, and the Moderator prays to God for ten minutes. Then he goes to worship other people. After lunch he sings hymns for half an hour, then prays for quarter of an hour. After tea he likes to relax by playing Trivial Pursuit while watching TV. For supper he has wine and toast and then goes to bed.' The ideas that some grown-ups have of parish ministers and what they do, is equally strange and far from the truth.

THE MINISTERS OF ST WITHIT

(Can be sung to the tune 'Tit Willow' from *The Mikado*)

Two sad little ministers languished and sighed,
    Get with it, Ah with it, Yea with it.
We hardly succeed though we've frequently tried
    To be with it, Ah with it, Yea with it.
We follow the fashion by leaps and by hops
    In spite of the fact that the chase never stops
To bring up the church to the top of the pops
    All with it, Ah with it, Yea with it.

The organ we've changed for a drum and guitar
    To be with it, Ah with it, Yea with it.
Paul McCartney we're signing on for the choir
    To be with it, Ah with it, Yea with it.
And now we've got rid of the sermon and creed
    To fall into line with the modern need
And morals from ancient restrictions we've freed
    To be with it, Ah with it, Yea with it.

The vestry and choir aisle we've made coffee stalls
   To be with it, Ah with it, Yea with it.
A Sunday night disco we hold in our halls
   To be with it, Ah with it, Yea with it.
We don't speak about clothes, we just have our gear
   To our elders' advice we turn a deaf ear
To be thought of as square is our greatest fear
   We'll be with it, Ah with it, Yea with it.

To keep up to date is a terrible strain
   If you're with it, Ah with it, Yea with it.
The Presbytery thinks we've gone insane
   Being with it, Ah with it, Yea with it.
The Session is getting exceedingly tough
   And the older guild ladies are cutting up rough
Though we find the reflection consoling enough
   That we're with it, Ah with it, Yea with it.

Our firm resolution no critic can shake
   To be with it, Ah with it, Yea with it.
And no opposition our spirit can break
   To be with it, Ah with it, Yea with it.
We'll follow the fashion wherever we're led
   Even were it to tell us to stand on our head
And we firmly intend till we tumble down dead
   To be with it, Ah with it, Yea with it.

When a visitor sentimentally remarked to the Rev Dr George Hodges that in Heaven there would be no partings, the busy dean replied tartly that what he hoped for was a place with no meetings.

My Native Land

Love for one's native land is as natural and normal as love of home and family. Rudyard Kipling wrote:

> God gives all men all earth to love
> But since man's heart is small
> Ordains for each one spot shall prove
> Beloved over all.

Drenched though Scotland sometimes is with rain; swirled though the Highlands often are with mountain mist, there is no other place I would rather live and work. When the sun shines – and it does more often than many think – the countryside is breathtaking, the wide horizons, glorious sunsets, golden beaches, the play of light and shade on the hills, the flaming yellow of the broom and whin in Spring, and the purple heather-covered mountains in the Autumn.

But ultimately it is not the landscape or the weather that sets the style of any country. It is her people. Out of Scotland's unique history of unremitting struggle, there has come strength and quality of character. Out of battles for great causes, have come self-reliance and genuine pride in all things Scottish. Adversity, righteousness and faith have exalted the Scottish nation. For the most part Scots don't feel snooty towards anyone else, but by the same token they have no feeling of inferiority either. Despite the common image of dour and mean Scots, they are in fact a fun-loving and very generous people. The dour Scot is often a secret sentimentalist, one who has great difficulty keeping the secret. There is no more hospitable nation in the world. As Robert Burns, our national bard, put it:

> When death's dark stream I ferry o'er
> A time that surely shall come
> In heaven itself I'll ask no more
> Than just a Highland welcome.

One of my favourite cartoons appeared in a newspaper at the time of the Battle of Britain. One Scot is saying to the other, 'You know Willie, if the English surrender we might have a bit of a fight on our hands.'

Andrew Carnegie tells in his autobiography how upset he was when a big boy at school told him that England was far larger than Scotland. His uncle sought to console him: 'Not at all, Andrew; if Scotland was rolled out as flat as England, Scotland would be larger, but would you really want the Highlands rolled flat?'

On the occasion of Carnegie being granted the Freedom of the City of Edinburgh, he said of his young American wife, 'Louise has found in Scotland all that she imagined of this country, exceeded tenfold. I begin to see in her the great danger that exists in all converts, she is beginning to out-Herod her husband in her love and devotion to Scotland.'

Laurie McMenemy, the former Manager of Southampton Football Club, once told Jock Stein that when his team won the FA Cup at Wembley, the people of the town decorated his house with flags and banners and put fairy lights on the streets. Jock, knowing how fickle football supporters could be, replied, 'Laurie, wait until you lose your next three games, the trees as well as the lights will come down.'

In a packed London tube train the emergency brakes suddenly went on. People were thrown in all directions. One Londoner got an elbow in his ribs, another an elbow in his face. Several were thrown to the ground. Many were bruised and irritated. Then suddenly as tempers were beginning to boil over, a man with a Scottish accent was heard to say, 'Unscheduled stop. All change for good nature.' There was a spontaneous burst of laughter.

William Chambers tells of a conversation he had with the Rev Sydney Smith. In reply to his comment that Mr Smith must have noticed that the Scots have a considerable fund of humour, Mr Smith replied, 'By all means. You are an immensely funny people, but you need a little operation to let the fun out. I know no instrument so effectual for the purpose as the corkscrew!'

There is a tale of an English officer who led a troop of Scottish soldiers out of the trenches in the Western desert. As they charged, the piper played *Scotland the Brave*, only to be met by a hail of bullets that sent them all scurrying for cover. 'We'll try again, chaps,' said the young officer. 'Only this time, piper, could you play something they like?'

An American who had been touring Scotland in the company of a Scottish relative, had been persistently belittling everything he saw. On the return journey to Edinburgh, the American glimpsed the magnificent Forth Rail Bridge. 'What's that?' said the American. Back came the brilliant reply: 'I don't know, it wasn't there last week.'

If you want the plain unvarnished truth, trust the Highlander to give instant delivery. An old Highland farmer decided to consult the new doctor who had arrived in the village. On hearing about this, his former doctor hastened to the farm. 'I hope this doesn't mean you are losing faith in me,' he said. 'Naw, naw,' reassured the old farmer, 'ye canna lose what you never had.'

There was also the Highlander who said to the newly inducted minister, 'If we like you we will say naught – but if we don't, we'll tell ye.'

Life in Dornoch can provide a marvellous contrast to the hustle of city living. Some years ago a visitor asked a local, 'What time do the Highland Games begin?' The local worthy smiled and said, 'When everybody's ready.'

A dour Scot who was due to retire after forty years working in the same railway signal-box, was being congratulated on his achievement: 'That's something of a record, forty years in the one box.' His reply was curt: 'I'll be longer in the next.'

A classic example of Scots composure is to be found in the reply of Mrs Baird, on receiving the news that her son David, who later became General Sir David Baird, was a prisoner in the hands of Hyder Ali. 'Lord help the lad that's chained tae oor Davie.'

I can think of many Scots who though they have lived abroad for many years have retained their Scottish accent. The reason for this is probably that they have never found a better one to change to.

The Scottish accent can sometimes present problems. An Englishman who was on a cycling tour of Scotland tells how he had just finished his sandwiches when a car pulled up. 'Would you like to eat out?' asked an old Scotsman as he lowered the window. The cyclist was puzzled by the question and declined, but the old man was not put off. 'Och come on. You wouldn't say no tae a wee bit o' Scottish hospitality.' With that, he thrust into his hand a plastic bag containing two gleaming, newly caught fish. As he drove off it dawned on the cyclist that the man had been saying, 'Would you like two wee trout?'

Scotsmen can sometimes get tongue-tied or confused in the presence of the famous. Professor William Barclay, who became a household name in Scotland as a result of his television broadcasts, loved to tell how a stranger once said to him, 'Dr Barclay, you're my greatest fan.'

The story is told of an army chaplain who got some Scottish soldiers to transform a vacant army hut into a little chapel. The soldiers accepted the challenge. On inspecting their work, the chaplain was somewhat taken aback to discover that they had painted above the pulpit the words, 'Scotland for Ever'. As tactfully as possible, he suggested that they might have chosen something a little more religious. 'You leave it to us padre,' they said. The following day when he returned, he discovered the inscription had been altered to read, 'Scotland for Ever and Ever, Amen'.

At the time of the Highland Clearances, the factors who ran Highland estates for the absentee landlords exercised great power. At times they could be ruthless. The memory of their heartless deeds lingers on. Not surprisingly a smile came over the faces of some worshippers when one Sunday morning, while reading from the Passion narrative, the assistant minister declared in sonorous tones, 'And there were also two male factors crucified with Jesus.'

Some Scottish sub-editors were once discussing what simple headlines would sell the most newspapers. The consensus of opinion was that none would beat, 'Pope Elopes'.

Brian Majoribanks had his first television role as a foot-baller in an episode of *Dr Finlay's Casebook*. He was a member of the Tannochbrae team. The filming was done at the Alloa Athletic football ground. The supporters were asked to wait behind at the close of the Saturday game. They were given the appropriate banners to wave and told to shout, 'Come on Tannochbrae.' The supporters were most obliging. Moments before they started filming, a female member of the crew came running over to Brian and started putting on make-up. Recalling later how the supporters suddenly began shouting, 'You big pansy!' Brian says, 'Could you blame them, especially with a surname like Marjoribanks.'

Old Joe who was 'fitba daft' ran a junior team in Kilsyth, called Kilsyth Emmett. He picked the team, repaired the boots and the nets, packed the hamper, cut the grass. He also often paid the bus fares. A friend, Bob Morrow, recalls one unforgettable piece of advice that Joe gave. It came just before his team took to the field to face a side renowned for their tough tackling. When one of his younger players asked whether they should retaliate if the other team started kicking them, Old Joe looked at the lad and then delivered the following gem, 'Ah think wi' this lot son, you'd be as well tae retaliate first!'

Bob Morrow also tells about a young footballer called McCallister who, as well as being a good full-back, was also a snooker expert. On one occasion he had his head shaved for some sponsored event. During the first hairless match which he played, he went up to head the ball clear. Unfortunately it skidded off his head into the net. Somebody shouted, 'For ony sake, McCallister – chalk yer cue!'

Andy Stewart, the Scottish singer and entertainer, told of an embarrassing experience. He had been invited to open a church Sale of Work. What he didn't know, was that in the congregation there was a strong temperance association. Having done various impersonations of how famous people might open the sale, he was just about to open the sale when a lady at the back of the hall shouted, 'Give us a song, Andy.' He obliged, but unfortunately the song he chose on the spur of the moment was *Campbeltown Loch*, with the lines, 'I wish you were whisky, for I would drink you dry'. The faces of some of the ladies got longer and longer, but having started he had to finish.

An English author had come North to find out what he could about the Highlands for a novel he was hoping to write. His hope was that by talking to the locals he would get the feel of the place. What he failed to realise was just how reticent West Coast folk can sometimes be with strangers. The first person he met was a gravedigger engaged in digging a grave. Standing at the edge of the grave he said to the gravedigger, 'Don't you find it cold up here?' Without looking up the gravedigger muttered, 'It's caulder doon here.' When he then asked, 'Do people die often up here?' the equally brief reply was, 'Just yince.' His third attempt was no more successful, 'Have you lived all your days here?' 'No yet,' the gravedigger replied.

At a Celtic-Motherwell match, one Celtic supporter, incensed at the referee awarding a penalty against his team, shouted, 'I wish your mother had been on the pill.'

A high-powered salesman from the South was anxious to get to one of the Outer Isles, clinch a business deal and get back the same day. He was one of the world's 'pushers', the kind of person who will go into a swing door behind you and come out in front of you. In the timetable the island ferry was scheduled to leave at twelve noon. But at noon there was, however, no sign of life about the ferry terminal. Half an hour later the ferryman had still not arrived. Becoming more and more irritated, he inquired as to the ferryman's possible whereabouts. Finding him in the local pub chatting to his friends, the salesman asked, with an urgent scowl on his face, when the ferry normally left. 'Oh sometimes we leave at twelve o'clock, sometimes at one o'clock, sometimes at two, and then of course sir, sometimes we're late!'

A London lady who had advertised for a maid, finally selected a capable Scots lass. After a few weeks the lady told her how pleased she was with her, then she added, 'One thing puzzles me. You didn't mention in your application that you were from Scotland. That surprises me, for most employers like Scottish girls. They have a reputation for being good workers. If you ever apply again for a job, mention it in your application.' 'But Ma'am,' said the girl, 'I was always taught it was bad manners to boast.'

After ten years in charge of the Scottish Civil Service, Sir Kerr Fraser was invited to become Principal of Glasgow University. When asked how the two jobs compared, he replied, 'In both there's far too much paper. I used to joke that my wife said of me, "A thousand pages in his sight, are but an evening gone."'

The Dear Green Place

Professor James Denney once said, 'I would rather be unhappy in Glasgow than happy anywhere else.' Many Glaswegians, myself included, feel like that about Glasgow. It keeps tugging at our heartstrings. Glasgow has fine concert halls, internationally famous museums and countless church spires dotting the skyline, but what makes Glasgow great are the people who live in its houses, work in its offices, walk its pavements and relax in its beautiful parks. During a visit to the city the Queen referred to 'the warm smile on Glasgow's face'. That was a legitimate generalisation. Friendly and often over-generous with money, the Glaswegian is the opposite of the Scottish stereotype of being 'mean' and 'dour'. Glaswegians are for the most part warm, down to earth folk, who quickly make strangers feel at home. If you ask a Glaswegian for directions, the strong likelihood is that instead of directing you, he will take you.

Glasgow today is a much changed place from the Glasgow St Mungo founded, 'that dear green place' by the Molendinar burn. It is a changed place too from the Glasgow of the tobacco lords, and the Glasgow of the busy shipyards. What world-beaters Glasgow ship-builders were. No longer is the ding-dong of the shipyard hammers the Song of the Clyde. Glasgow's story continues to be the seesaw it has always been. Once again, out of the ashes has come a fine, new and attractive city. Most of the old Glasgow slums have gone. Many of the extraordinary Victorian buildings with their marvellously useless decorative façades have been given a facelift and floodlit. Who would have guessed even a decade before that distinguished Eurocrats would vote Glasgow, European City of Culture in 1990. The fact that this should have happened is tribute to Glasgow's amazing powers of renewal.

For better or worse Glasgow helped make me the person I am. In its busy city streets I learned to be a suicidal jay-walker. To Glasgow I owe my love of fun and humour. Her jovial people are among the natural comics of the world. It was at Glasgow University that I studied science and later divinity. (There is no truth in the rumour that whereas Edinburgh was the theological centre of the Old World, and Princeton in America the theological centre of the New World, Glasgow University was the theological centre of the Underworld.) It was in its Cathedral that I was licensed to do what the city motto reminds us is the secret of the city's greatness – to preach the Word. 'Let Glasgow flourish by the preaching of the Word.'

I am proud to be a Glaswegian.

Two Glasgow men were standing at the street corner, helping to support the tenement building, when a lorry passed laden to the brim with beautiful turf. 'How would you like to be that rich,' said one to the other, 'that you could send your grass away for cutting?'

The advocate who in the Glasgow High Court was defending the accused was well known for his ability in court, and also for the fact that he spent most of his time in the city's pubs and hotel bars. At one point in the trial the advocate said, 'Your honour, just let me draw an analogy. It is just as if I saw you going into a pub.' At this point the judge interrupted, 'For the sake of accuracy, don't you mean *coming* in?'

The Very Rev Andrew Doig told how shortly after his retiral, he boarded a Glasgow bus and asked the cheery driver if it went to the University. 'Yes, young fellow, welcome aboard,' he replied. 'Less of the young fellow,' said Dr Doig. 'It's a long time since I was at the University.' Being an exact change bus, he got no change from his 50p for his 40p ticket. 'The other 10p is your donation to the deserving poor,' he was told. Ten minutes later as he got off the bus, the driver, perhaps seeking to make amends, said, 'Well cheerio. It's always a pleasure to give the Principal of the University a lift.'

Two Glasgow men, chatting over the garden fence, suddenly saw a hearse go by. 'Wha's deid?' asked one. 'Him in the box,' said the other. 'Aye,' mused the first, 'the driver looked OK.'

Over a stall at the Barrows (a Glasgow open-air market) where duvet covers were on sale, there was a notice: 'Feather-filled duvets. Buy now before the price of down goes up.'

In the Glasgow University Union there was a notice asking for names of those interested in playing football for the University. The notice had three columns: Name, Address, Position. The first name to be appended was: John the Baptist; the Wilderness, Jordan; Desperate.'

Returning one day from Glasgow on the Inverness train, I had on sports jacket and flannels. The train was full of men returning to the oil rig construction yard at Kishorn in Wester Ross. The friendly Glasgow man opposite me produced his quarter bottle of whisky and offered me a drink – or what is known in Glasgow as a 'slug'. I graciously declined. Shortly afterwards he leant across and said, 'How long have you worked at

Kishorn?' When I informed him that I did not work there, he said, 'What do you do?' When I told him I was a Church of Scotland minister, he said, 'Oh my Goad.' I was very tempted to say, 'You flatter me.'

In a bus queue, whipped by an arctic wind, a little old Glasgow woman saw the misery of some American tourists. 'You have to be born here to live here,' she said.

A Glaswegian tells how one winter's night, the attractive girl sitting beside him in the bus was obviously feeling the cold, so she closed the window above her. A moment later the person behind her opened it. A few moments later she closed it. This happened a few more times, until she turned round and demanded in exasperation, 'What do you think you are playing at?' The young man replied with a grin, 'Draughts – it's your move.'

Alistair Macdonald, the singer and broadcaster, tells of a brief encounter as he walked up Byres Road in Glasgow. A dear old lady approached him. 'It is you, isn't it?' she said. Certain that she had recognised him from his TV appearance the previous night, he replied, 'Yes it is.' He was, however, duly humbled when she then demanded, 'When are you coming to finish painting my kitchen?'

Dr Andrew Herron, one of Glasgow's best known ministers, told of a Glasgow lady who proudly announced to her husband that their daughter was 'going steady with an awfully nice boy whose people are in iron and steel.' 'Oh aye,' said her man, 'I ken the faimly fine, his mither does the ironin' an his faither does the stealin'!' 'So much,' says Dr Herron, 'for "Glasgow culture".'

Gerard Kelly the actor remembers how during a period of severe unemployment in Scotland, he was taking part in the filming of a scene for a television play. All the lights and cameras were set up in front of a Glasgow Job Centre. During a break in the filming, a Glasgow man who was passing, said, 'What's the big event? Has somebody actually got a job?'

The Rev James Currie was one of Glasgow's best after-dinner speakers. He spoke at so many Burns Suppers that some people thought he had invented them. His biographer tells how at one golf club Burns Supper, the proceedings were delayed because there was an unexpected shortage of seats. Apparently some tickets had been forged! That night James began his Immortal Memory by saying, 'I have taken some people to court, but this is the first time I have driven them to crime.'

Another great pastime of James Currie's was taking people on tours of the Holy Land. On one occasion on the return journey, one of the ladies on the tour suffered heart pains. Landing in Glasgow, he went with her in the ambulance to the hospital. There he overheard the doctor ask, 'Is Mr Currie your minister?' To his embarrassment the woman replied, 'No, he's just the man I've been on holiday with.'

A Glasgow butcher used to say to those who appeared in his shop after a holiday, 'I hope you're nane the waur o' yer holiday.' The possibility that they might be the better for it did not seem to enter his mind.

A Glasgow couple saved up for years to go on a cruise when the husband retired. They decided to travel first class. Shortly after they set sail, a cabin boy came along and invited them to sit at the chief engineer's table. 'Well I never,' said his wife. 'Just because we're from Glasgow they want us to muck in with the crew!'

A woman was heard telling her pals in Glasgow's West End, 'My husband had a near-death experience at the weekend. He tried to change the channel when *Strictly Come Dancing* was on.'

A Mr Mortimer was shopping in a Glasgow department store and overheard a young assistant trying to sell an expensive doll to a woman with two small daughters in tow. 'It walks and talks,' she explained, 'and when you put it down it shuts its eyes and goes to sleep just like a real baby.' 'I can see,' replied the customer, 'that you don't know much about real babies.'

James Arthur tells how he was standing on the terracing at Easter Road football ground awaiting the start of a Hibs-Rangers match when two Glasgow supporters appeared beside him. One of them, seemingly there for the first time, gazed around and exclaimed, 'Here, Pe'er, this isnae much o' a grun, is it?' 'Ah but see Willie,' his pal replied, 'ye huv tae make allooances – we're in ra provinces.'

The British Open at Troon in the early 1960s was won by Arnold Palmer. All week he had been hitting the ball prodigious distances. A Glasgow man who was greatly impressed, turned to his wife, as the drive once more went screaming off into the heavens: 'Jeannie, that man hits his drives further than we go on wur holidays.'

The following conversation was overheard in a Glasgow electrical shop: 'Have you anything I can fit to my television that will interfere with my neighbour's electric drill?'

A Glasgow man was heard to say, 'My wife's the double of Kate Moss. Kate is 8 stone, my wife is 16.'

On leaving the restaurant, the stranger was addressed by a little Glasgow man. 'Excuse me, are you Jimmy Scott?' 'No,' replied the stranger. 'Well I am, and you're wearing his coat.'

Yet another Glasgow man was overheard saying, 'Jimmy is the kind of guy who if you lent him £1,000 and then did not see him again for five years, you would think, "That was money well spent".'

Shortly after the Glasgow police had started a major recruiting campaign to attract people from the city's ethnic minorities, a beautiful young Indian girl graduate applied. The officer in charge of recruitment decided to give her application and recruitment maximum publicity. The press were invited to meet her. One photographer asked if they could be allowed to photograph her with a police motorcyclist. The policeman chosen had a face as weatherbeaten as Ben Cruachan. He had served as a constable in the force for twenty-five years. Once the photographers had got their pictures, he was asked by one reporter how he felt about this young Indian girl graduate joining the force. 'It's great,' he said, 'I've always maintained that what is wrong wi' the Glasgow police force is that there are far too many chiefs and no enough Indians.'

At a professional boxing match at Shawfield in the thirties the participants were Len Harvey, a one-time British Middleweight Champion, and another boxer from Leith. The ring was lit by arc lamps and the fight had gone two or three rounds with little to excite the crowd, both men apparently still sizing one another up.

The spectators were getting a little impatient when suddenly a voice roared out, 'Aw, pit oot the lights!' From another quarter came a swift reply, 'Aw, dinnae pit oot the lights – I'm readin ma paper.' At this point the fight really started and then came another call from somewhere in the crowd, 'Send fur the polis, there's twa men gonnae fight!'

The story is told of a Glasgow man who was posted for a short spell of duty in London. On his return home he was asked how he had found the English. 'I didn't meet many,' he replied. 'You see, I was only dealing with heads of departments and most of them were Scots.'

There is a shaft of Glasgow anti-intellectualism in one of James Bridie's comedies. The mistress of the house is scolding the Glasgow maid for the untidy state of the rooms. 'Look,' she says, 'I can write my name in the dust.' To which comes the withering reply, 'It's a great thing education.'

The Royal Artillery Band was playing one night in an open-air bandstand of a Glasgow park. It was a pouring wet night. Their audience consisted of only one man, who sat huddled in a deck chair, getting more and more drenched, and showing little reaction to their music. Finally the band sergeant went and asked him if he had a special request. The man replied that he did. 'I would like this concert to end as soon as possible. I'd like to lock the gates and go home.'

Royal and Ancient

It is not surprising that the game of golf, as we know it, began in Scotland, for so much of our Scottish coastline is natural golfing country. The ancient dunes, carpeted with centuries-old turf, broken by erosion here and there into sand traps, made perfect golfing territory.

There are a few Scottish golf clubs where one would probably have to be knighted before being considered for membership, but fortunately there are not too many. In rural and seaside communities, golf has long been accessible to all. When I came to Dornoch in the 1970s and joined my three sons as members of the world-famous Royal Dornoch Golf Club, reckoned to be one of the twelve top courses in the world, I got change out of a pound! The annual subscription for a local junior was then 25p. At that time I had some difficulty convincing my golfing friends in Glasgow that the call to Dornoch actually came from the Cathedral and not from the Royal Dornoch Golf Club.

In my teenage years I took golf far too seriously. I thought, dreamt and spoke of little else. That has changed. Today I know what golf spells backwards! Now it is the social aspect of the game, the chat, the good-natured banter and the friendly competition that I find most appealing. Golf is a pleasant game, played in God's out of doors, mostly by pleasant people, who are often at their most pleasant when among fellow golfers. If in a match with family and friends, I can achieve a few pars and experience the thrill of the occasional birdie, then Whoopee!... but if I don't, it's no longer the end of the world.

Golf affords healthy exercise, sweeps away mental cobwebs, and offers challenge and excitement How we play reveals something of our character. How we lose reveals even more.

Golf is a game in which a ball 1½ inches in diameter is placed on a ball 8,000 miles in diameter, the object being to hit the small ball before you hit the big one.

Golf is a game that is played by many men to keep them from falling asleep in church on Sunday mornings.

'Golf,' said Churchill, 'is a game designed by the devil and played with instruments ill-adapted for the purpose.'

Golf is a lot of walking broken up by disappointment and bad arithmetic.

Golf is a game that consists of a hundred or more neurological spasms – called shots – involving fourteen clubs and sometimes quite a number of golf balls. It involves a plethora of twanging nerves and a small amount of skill.

Golf is a game introduced centuries ago by a Scottish sadist to drive generations insane with disappointment, for almost everything a golfer does falls into three categories: slightly wrong, wrong and disastrous. At the end of the 19th century, other sadistic Scots exported the game. Having themselves been driven mad by missed short putts and duffed drives, they were determined to make foreigners suicidal too.

Golf is a game in which grown men and women flog, flail and fracture a green landscape on which eighteen holes are hidden in satanic design.

Golf is also a great leveller. The bank director often takes three to get down from two yards. The prime minister and president, with the fate of nations in their hands, are still subject to the shank. A Scottish PGA starter tells how at Pro-Ams, highly paid executives will approach him and quietly whisper, 'When my turn comes, don't bother announcing my name.' One was so nervous he had to use two hands to tee up the ball. Another, who kept running to the toilet, finally confessed he now knew the colour of adrenalin!

Sandy Matheson was one of the characters in the Royal Dornoch Golf Club. The members and visitors for whom he caddied loved his lively wit. One year in the 3-man team tournament, in which the best two scores count, my sons had been out early. They had both returned net 66s over the championship course. By comparison, I had a poor round. When I joined them later in the clubhouse, Sandy, well aware of my sons' low scores, and my much higher one, turned to the local doctor, and in a voice loud enough for all in the clubhouse to hear, said, 'It's well seen the minister's sons have not been studying the Epistle of *James.*'

The first thing you have to learn is how to tell a No.6 iron from a No.9 upside down.

Whereas to 'put' is to place a thing where you want it, to 'putt' is a vain attempt to do the same thing.

There is no truth in the idea that the saying, 'Take off your shoes for the place whereon you are standing is holy ground' was first spoken by a golf club secretary to a member who had spikes on in the clubhouse lounge.

With many golfers there is an enormous ration of talk to skill. The fact that a person has succumbed to golf mania is generally manifested in his speech. He begins to talk in a strange tongue, about hazards and bunkers and bogeys and pars. In describing a recent game, no incident is omitted. With painful minuteness he reconstructs the entire round. He talks endlessly about the lies he had – or perhaps lies about his lies. The golfing enthusiast's prayer to the patron saint of golf, highlights this strong temptation:

> From the many bad lies upon the links
> St Andrew guard me still
> From the lie in the sand and the muddy lie
> And the lie on the sloping hill;
> From the lie in the whins and the stony lie
> And the lie of the golfing bore;
> But of all the bad lies I pray thee grace
> From the lie about my score.

When a man who had failed to break a hundred said, 'That really is not my normal game,' his more honest partner said, 'I haven't been on my normal game for thirty years.' I like that. I also like the remark made by a man with whom I once golfed for the first time. He did not play well, yet despite this, thoroughly enjoyed the game. As we finished he said, 'No matter how I talk about golf and dream about it, that is the way I play.' What refreshing honesty.

If the gaping bunkers at the second hole in Dornoch could speak, they would afford glorious entertainment. It was there I once listened to a gentleman of position and education holding an animated conversation with his little white ball, finally committing its poor soulless body to imperishable flames.

A stomach specialist has a simple formula for disposing of patients with nervous indigestion. He asks them if they play golf. If they say 'Yes', he orders them to stop. If they say 'No', he orders them to start.

At Balmoral Castle, the Queen's holiday residence in Scotland, there is an attractive nine-hole golf course. On one side of the first hole is a statue of Queen Victoria. On the other side of the ninth fairway there is a statue of her husband Prince Albert. When I first saw these statues of a husband and a wife separated by a golf course, I suspected there was a parable there somewhere.

H V Morton in his book *In Search of Scotland* tells of a man in a hotel in St Andrews. He practised golf shots with his soup spoon. When the soup course was over he would practise his putting across the tablecloth by hitting bread pellets with a fork. Morton was sure this plus-foured oddity was the same man who occupied the bedroom next to his and continued his golfing dream throughout the night. 'Even his snore sounded like Fore!'

A doctor once received a phone-call asking if he could make up a foursome at golf. Having intimated that he would be straight over, he put down the phone. As his sympathetic wife got his coat and medical bag, she enquired if it was important. 'I'm afraid it is my dear, there are three doctors there already.'

The ultimate demonstration of unpopularity is the player who phoned a neighbour to suggest a game on Saturday, to be told, 'Sorry, we already have a three.'

'What do you mean you played Second World War golf?' a man asked his friend in the clubhouse bar. The friend replied, 'Out in 39 and back in 45.'

Bob Hope used to tell how he had a wonderful short game, but unfortunately it was off the tee. 'Never before has anyone swung so hard for so little.'

The Scot Eric Brown was one of the few British golfers in the 1950s to have no fear of a head-to-head confrontation with any American. When he was told in 1953 that he had been chosen for the Ryder Cup team, his brief comment was, 'We're one up.'

The 6th hole at Royal Dornoch is one of the most difficult par 3 holes in golf. A local who had nightmares about this hole once said that the easiest way to take eight strokes off his score, was simply to omit the 6th.

The golf shots which Alan Shepard hit on the moon with a five iron will long be recalled in the history of sport. The madness of golfers had surfaced again. For the sake of a few golf shots, this 12 handicap golfer risked a billion-dollar disaster by doing what might have torn his life-support suit. I wonder if he risked all to fulfil every golfer's dream. When Alan's great cry came down from the moon, 'It is sailing for miles and miles,' was he not voicing the hidden desire of most golfers to do just that?

A golf fanatic said of Arnold Palmer, 'He has won as much money as I have spent on golf lessons.'

A Morag Ross tells how her six-year-old son was very concerned to see her taking two paracetamol tablets to ease a strained back prior to the final of our golf club ladies championship. 'Won't you fail the drug test if you win?' he asked.

A golf widow had learned not to expect her husband to remember special dates but it was too much to take when he celebrated 18 years of marriage by playing 18 holes of golf. When she expressed her dismay at his forgetfulness, he exclaimed, 'Darling! I did NOT forget. I told everyone on the golf course that today is my anniversary.'

How did they measure hail before the golf ball was invented?

A dentist with a passion for golf left a message with the receptionist that he was to be away all morning and that she should give her usual reply to any enquiries. Rather tired, however, of covering for her truant boss, when one of his regular patients asked to see him, she modified the stock reply by saying, 'I'm sorry, Madam. I'm afraid he is out on a special case. He has 18 cavities to fill and he says it will take him all morning.'

When asked to define the most difficult shot in golf, Groucho Marx raised his eyebrows, tipped imaginary ash from his unlit Havana cigar and replied, 'I find it to be the hole in one.'

The putt has been defined as a tender shot played on the green, usually followed by anguished eyes directed heavenwards; the fairway as the well-kept but seldom-used part of the course.

Henry Longhurst, the famous golf commentator and writer, tells how he believes he was the first to discover that, as the average golf club weighs approximately 13–14 oz, a full set of fourteen clubs weighs less than a stone. 'So when I weigh in at 15 stone, I am carrying the equivalent of 60 wooden clubs, 150 irons and more than 100 golf balls.' He once shared this interesting, but rather useless piece of information, with a rather overweight friend of his, Lord Banbury. The next time they met the noble Lord informed Henry Longhurst with considerable pride that his bathroom scales that morning had revealed that he had lost all his irons and two of his woods.

A favourite golfing story of Henry Longhurst concerned a vicar who took an enormous divot out of the sacred turf. 'Shall I put it back?' his caddie asked respectfully, 'or will you keep it for the harvest festival?'

A weekend golfer, plagued with nerves whenever he had a card in his hand, was given a tranquilliser by his wife. She told him to put it in his shirt pocket and take it just before the game. Afterwards she marvelled as he recounted how he had sunk impossible putts to win the tournament. Then she noticed something in his pocket, fished it out and said, 'But you forgot to take the tranquilliser.' It was then her husband realised he had played his greatest game on a button he had put in the same pocket after it fell off his shirt.

The late Justice McKenna of the United States Supreme Court was an earnest but rather poor golfer. Deciding that his game might be improved, he hired an instructor to teach him the finer points. One day, while practising on a golf course near Washington, he missed the ball. He tried three or four times, but each time his club hit several inches behind the ball. His instructor watched silently. Finally the Justice, becoming disgusted, glared at the still stationary ball and muttered, 'Tut tut.' Gravely the instructor walked towards him. 'Sir,' he said, 'you will never learn to play golf with these words.'

I was fortunate in being present at the dinner in the Pinehurst Hotel when the former Open Champion Roberto de Vicenzo was introduced to the World Golf Hall of Fame. That night he told how when he first started playing in American tournaments, he knew no

English. His English he learned from the professionals with whom he played. He recalled that it was some time before he realised that certain words that he had picked up from his fellow professionals, were not words you used in polite company!

At one part of the course there was a fast-flowing stream. Having driven across it, a Scot turned to his friend and said with glee, 'Yon's a bonnie wee burn.' But the following week when he failed to clear it, he was heard to shout, 'That damned sewer.'

A lady member of Airdrie Golf Club phoned the *Herald* sports department their May competition results, including who had won the May Cup. She was not amused when it appeared the following day in the newspaper as the Makeup winner.

A professional was once asked to give a very wealthy and famous person a lesson. He began by asking the important man to hit a few balls. Having seen his swing, he then made a few suggestions as to how it could be improved, but each time he said anything, the VIP interrupted him with his own version of what was wrong and how he should correct it. After this had happened a few times the professional simply began nodding in agreement. At the end of the lesson the man paid the professional and complimented him on what a fine teacher he was. Later that day, a member of the club who had been standing on the practice range, near to where the professional was giving the lesson, said to him, 'That was an amazing performance this afternoon. Why did you finally just agree with the nonsense that man was talking?' 'Well,' said the old professional, 'I learned a long time ago that it was a waste of time trying to sell answers to a man who only wants to buy echoes.'

A lady tells how her husband's joyful anticipation of his golfing holiday was almost more than she could bear. For weeks before the foursome left, he practised putting, chipping and driving. In between he polished his clubs, bag and shoes. 'I get the impression,' she finally said, 'that you are looking forward to this trip more than you looked forward to our wedding.' 'Well, that was only one day,' he replied, 'this is three!'

The Glasgow Golf Club 'Minutes' record how during the Second World War a minister who was a member of the council had proposed that as an act of solidarity with those fighting in the war, the members should agree to abstain from drinking alcohol in the clubhouse. The minute goes on to tell how 'the motion was discussed and found to be lacking in merit'.

Bing Crosby died while playing golf. The Radio Clyde producer, wanting to be the first to broadcast the news, interrupted the record programme and announced Bing's death. Wanting to follow the announcement with a record, he reached for one by the old crooner. His embarrassment was considerable when he discovered the one he had put on the turntable was *Cheek to Cheek*, which starts: Heaven, I'm in heaven...

Lee Trevino, at one stage in his 40s, contemplated retiring. He credits his wife with keeping him in the game. 'She kept telling me I could win. She'd say, "Those clubs of yours don't have any idea how old you are".'

The following note was left in the Suggestion Box of a Scottish Golf Club: 'Hasn't the Committee's two-year experiment of having no plug in the middle wash-hand basin in the men's toilet, been given a long enough trial?'

A member raced back to the clubhouse from a lone practice round to announce excitedly, 'I've just had a hole in one at the 17th, and I've left the ball in the hole to prove it!'

Golf is one of God's greatest allies for keeping us humble. One day we think we have finally mastered it, the next we cannot do a thing right. At Rancho Park in Los Angeles, Arnold Palmer hit four consecutive shots out of bounds and wound up with a 12. When asked by a reporter how he had made a 12 on a par-five hole, Palmer replied, 'I missed a five-foot putt for an 11.'

Pope John Paul visited New York in 1979. The Mayor, along with other dignitaries, was at the airport to meet him. Just prior to his arrival, there was a tremendous thunderstorm, but as soon as the Pope stepped off the plane, the sun came out. A security officer next to the Mayor was heard to say, 'Now that's the kind of guy you want to have for a golf partner.'

The flamboyant Walter Hagen said he never wanted to be a millionaire, just to live like one! In the days when professionals were often not allowed into the clubhouse, he would change into his golf attire in a Rolls Royce parked in front of the clubhouse.

After a disastrous round of golf, a man was overheard to lament, 'Golf is a terrible game. I am glad I don't have to play it again until tomorrow.'

Golf finds fascinating ways to engage us, instruct us, cajole us, tease us, entertain us, enrage us and regularly defeat us.

A Chisel in my Hand

When a visitor to a local art exhibition inquired whether a certain painting was of a sunrise or a sunset, a girl standing near him said, 'It's a sunset. I know the painter. He never gets up early enough to paint a sunrise!'

I am not one either for rising at the crack of dawn, but I am grateful that when I do get up I not only have work to do, but work that I enjoy doing. Not all are as privileged.

Bishop Henson once told a group of coalminers in his diocese how he worked fourteen hours a day and asked for nothing better. The comment of one miner was, 'If I were a bishop, I too might work fourteen hours a day, but eight hours of my kind of work, with all the dirt, noise and sweat, is quite enough.'

In the caring and teaching professions, a great deal is said today about burn-out. It is a major problem. (Mark you, I sometimes wonder whether a few of those who claim to suffer from burn-out have ever been lit.) The stresses of work can be considerable but what of the stresses of unemployment? Some time ago an advert appeared in a Belfast newspaper: 'I am very keen to learn a trade. My parents are willing to pay if necessary. Would any kind, patient person help me. I am tall, strong and alert.' The psychological damage of having no meaningful work experience is considerable, for in the minds of many, a person's work and identity are closely linked. Recall how often we ask a stranger, 'What do you do?' Little wonder unemployed people feel a loss of dignity.

'It is well with me,' said Michelangelo, 'when I have a chisel in my hand.' Those of us who have a congenial and fulfilling job are indeed fortunate.

The closest to perfection many of us will ever get is when we fill in a job application.

Always put off until tomorrow that which you should not do at all.

I wonder what excuses people gave at work for their mistakes, before there were computers?

The size of the cut you inflict on yourself while shaving, is directly proportional to the importance of the interview, or event for which you are shaving.

Holidays should last long enough for your boss to miss you, but not long enough for him to discover that he can do without you.

Keep your sense of humour about your position at work, for, 'The higher a monkey climbs, the more you see of his behind!'

The engineering department of a large oil company is known for its good-looking secretaries. The motto is, 'Hire them and we will teach them to type.' One day a handsome young man came into the office seeking a job. During the interview the manager's secretary interrupted him to place a note on his desk: 'Hire him. We will teach him engineering.'

At the wedding of a computer programmer to a girl who was a computer operator, one telegram read, 'Now is the time to abandon your computers and learn to multiply in the good old-fashioned way.'

Indira Gandhi, the former Prime Minister, often quoted advice given to her early in life, by her grandfather,

Motilal Nehru: 'He told me there were two kinds of people – those who do the work of the world and those who take the credit. He said to try and be in the first group since there was much less competition there.'

Research is to see what everyone else has seen and to think what nobody else has thought.

'I'm not really late,' said the office-worker as she hung up her coat, 'I just took my coffee break before coming in.'

Harper Lee, who wrote *To Kill a Mockingbird*, did much of her creative thinking while golfing. 'If people know you are working at home,' she explained, 'they think nothing of calling in for coffee. But they wouldn't dream of interrupting you on the golf course.'

To get real enjoyment out of a garden, put on a straw hat, dress in old clothes, hold a trowel in one hand and a cool drink in the other, and tell the man where to dig.

When Pope John XXIII was asked how many people worked in the Vatican, he replied, with his usual sense of good humour, 'About half.'

In one application submitted to an employment agency, in answer to the question, 'Position desired', the applicant had written, 'Sitting'.

When John Glenn was asked to share some of his thoughts while orbiting the earth in *Friendship VII*, he said, 'I just kept looking at all these instruments and thinking how they were all supplied by the lowest bidder.'

Two ushers at the orchestral concert were loudly clapping at the end. They kept on and on. Those in the audience who were standing near them were somewhat disillusioned when they heard one say to the other, 'Another two minutes and we'll be in overtime.'

As part of an economy drive during the war, many communications had 'USE LESS PAPER' typed on the top left-hand corner of every page. This caused unforeseen problems. One clerk when asked to produce a certain letter replied that he had thrown it away. He explained that it had 'USELESS PAPER' written on it.

Nothing cures insomnia like the realisation that it is time to get up for work.

Manager to apprentice: 'We've done more for you than your mother ever did. We have carried you for fifteen months.'

Another manager who had been asked for a testimonial for the poorest worker he had ever known, found himself in a dilemma. He would fain have had the man leave, but such was his integrity that he refused to lie in the testimonial. The testimonial finally read, 'If you get this person to work for you, you will indeed be fortunate. And I'm sure if you decide to employ him, he will be fired with enthusiasm.'

Boss to worker: 'Don't think of it as a cut in salary. Think of it as another blow struck in the neverending fight against inflation.'

In a fascinating talk about bread making, a director of a large bread-making company told how, when he began in the bread business, there was a bakery in almost every fifth street. When he retired fifty years later, his factory employed only four engineers and a secretary. He shed light in his talk on the origin of such terms as 'society's upper crust' and speaking with 'a pan loaf accent'. The upper crust being the most nutritious part of the loaf, it was served to the top-table guests. And because for many years pan loaves were manufactured only in England and not Scotland, this gave rise north of the border to the phrase 'a pan loaf accent' to describe a posh English accent.

Notice on building site: 'Warning – Night Watchman patrols this area twenty-four hours a day.'

A monastery that was struggling financially decided as part of a fund-raising effort to open a 'carry out' within the monastery grounds. One night a new customer said to the monk working behind the counter, 'Are you the fish friar?' 'No,' he said, 'I am the chip monk!'

Chalked kerbside notice: 'The gas company are coming.' Someone had added, 'So is Christmas. Watch this space and see who arrives first'

A recently retired Edinburgh schoolteacher was reading the directions on the medicine bottle. At the foot of the label was the safety warning, 'Keep away from children'. 'Ah,' he said, 'if only somebody had given me that advice forty years ago.'

Sitting an IQ test were a banker, an electrician and a politician. One of the questions was, 'What term would you use to describe the problem that results when outflow exceeds inflow?' The banker wrote, 'Overdraft', the electrician wrote, 'Overload', and the politician wrote, 'What problem?'

A man who had gone privately to a psychiatrist was finally diagnosed as a workaholic. He had to take a second job to pay for the therapy!

Charles Clayton, an American professor of journalism, is convinced that newspapermen are the one profession that are sure to be found in heaven. He explains: 'They won't need doctors in heaven. Nobody will ever be ill. They won't need preachers. Everybody will already have been saved. But people in the south end of heaven will want to know what the people in the north end are doing, so they will need newspapermen.'

A Scottish farmer was approached by a former ploughman who said he was on the trail of a job and wondered whether he would give him a 'character reference'. 'Oh I could gie ye that,' said the farmer, 'but I think ye might manage better withoot it.'

Elizabeth Thomson employed removers to take her grand piano from the first floor down to the ground floor. They got stuck halfway down the stairs. As she stood sympathetically looking on, one of the men who was being gradually flattened by the wedged piano, looked at her and gasped, 'Couldn't you have played the flute instead?'

'You haven't even lifted the bonnet,' a driver complained to the garage mechanic estimating repair costs, 'how can you tell how much it's going to cost without looking at the engine?' 'I go by sounds,' said the mechanic, 'and that sound there costs two hundred quid to get rid of.'

James Fergusson tells of an elderly spinster who complained to a builder that his men had used awful language outside her house. The foreman denied this. On being asked to state exactly what occurred, he said, 'I accidentally let some hot lead fall off the scaffolding. Some of it went down Bill's neck and he called out, "You really ought to be more careful, Harry".'

Why do people retire, especially if they are not required to. The following have been suggested as possible reasons:

The carpet dealer: because he had made a pile.
The forester: because he got the axe.
The insurance agent: as a matter of policy.
The marriage counsellor: because he had worn his insights out.
The cook: because he was fed up.
The vet: because he was dog-tired.

'This car,' said a used car dealer, 'has low mileage.' The man selling it explained that he only drove it when he could get it started.

Man in underground train during the rush hour to fellow passenger. 'I have a job with a real challenge – getting to and from work every day.'

Customer to second-hand car salesman: 'What I'd really like is a car that runs as smoothly as you talk.'

The price of wood has got so ridiculous it's hard to believe it grows on trees!

A small businessman once said that for him two of the most beautiful words in the English language, are the words, 'Cheque enclosed'.

A lecturer in business studies reminded his students that 'Education is when you read the fine print. Experience is what you get when you don't.'

It's a pity that all the people who know how to run the country are either driving taxis or cutting hair.

Also by James A. Simpson from Steve Savage Publishers

Holy Wit   ISBN 9781904246022 RRP £4.99
'A really happy little book'
Northern Times

Laughter Lines   ISBN 9781904246282 RRP £4.95
'Crammed with jokes, aphorisms and humorous
anecdotes'
The Scotsman

Life, Love and Laughter   ISBN 9781904246046 RRP £5.99
'Full of cracking anecdotes'
Sunday Post

A Funny Way of Being Serious   ISBN 9781904246176 RRP £5.99
'Vintage Simpson – humour, insight, spiritual insight
and sacred comment'
Presbyterian Herald

At Our Age   ISBN 9781904246343 RRP £5.95
'A glorious collection of pieces related to getting older
... excellent as a gift at any time and not just for the
elderly'
The GoodBookstall

The Magic of Words   ISBN 9781904246411 RRP £4.95
'Dr Simpson's compassionate and humorous books ...
lift the spirits of all who read them'
The Herald

Available from bookshops or directly from the
publisher.

For information on mail order terms, see our website
(www.savagepublishers.com) or write to: Mail Order
Dept., Steve Savage Publishers Ltd., The Old Truman
Brewery, 91 Brick Lane, LONDON, E1 6QL